FROM
HELL TO
HEAVEN

From Surviving the Killing
Fields in Cambodia to the
Beatitudes of Living in Gratitude

SOPHAL PETTIT

Editor: Becky Norwood

Cover: Angie Analya
Interior Layout: Anna Goldsworthy

Disclaimer: ALL INFORMATION CONTAINED in this book is
intended for your general knowledge and the story is related by
Sophal Pettit, as she and her family experienced it. Any
similarities to situations and experiences are purely
coincidental.

From Hell to Heaven – From Surviving the Killing Fields of
Cambodia to the Beatitudes of Living in Gratitude Sophal Pettit

Website: www.sophalpettit.com

I

Table of Contents

Endorsement

This must-read book is a riveting, inspiring true story of survival, courage, and perseverance against tremendous odds and oppression.

I was so moved by *"From Hell to Heaven"*. Sophal Pettit seamlessly knits together the past and the present as she recounts living the horrors of war as a child, and then learns to rise above adversity as an adult with faith, hope, and forgiveness.

From *Hell to Heaven...* affirms our hope that the present can redeem the past and that God's love has the power to heal.

It is a poignant and memorable story of a war-torn family's rise from being victims of war, to living a life of victory. It is my honor and privilege to recommend and endorse this book.

Susan Miller, author of *After the Boxes Are Unpacked*
Founder and President, Just Moved Ministry

Dedication

I dedicate this book to God, my parents, husband, and my family. Also, to our families who died unjustly (grandma, aunties, uncles, cousins along with all the two million–plus people killed by the Pol Pot regime). This book, without God's blessing me with the wisdom to write, and then blessing me with an amazing publisher who spent countless hours editing to make this readable, would not have been completed. Thank you!

My parents, for their amazing loving hearts. They are willing to help anyone and everyone who comes to them for help, including their enemy. Not that they have a lot of money, they simply would give the shirt off their backs to help others. They are truly an example of what God means when he says to "love your enemy." They've consistently set an example and have shown me what it means to be content and filled with trust because we will always have enough. Somehow, someway, God will provide and always does. They are living examples of what it means to work hard, be grateful, and enjoy life along the way. You don't have to do the job you love, but you must love the job you have.

Most importantly this book is dedicated to my amazing husband, whose patience and belief in me throughout this journey has given me the confidence and will to learn and grow. (Thank you, honey!) Although the road we were on was rough our love was so much stronger. It made the journey worthwhile. It has been a wonderful journey! I am so blessed to have you in my life. When we started out, it was such a challenging and difficult journey for us, yet that's the road we chose. Through it all, I wouldn't change a thing. Our lives are like a roller coaster and it has been an exciting journey. You and I had all the odds against us, and yet continue to love and cherish each other. We have found a way to form a two-handed circle in our marriage with God in the center. No one can enter our circle, nor intercede and break the circle. Every day I love you more, for the man that you have become. We are so opposite from each other, and that's what makes it exciting, and why we continue growing our relationship. We are imperfectly perfect for each other. I could never ask for a better husband and partner in everything in my life. I thank you and I love you so much!

To my children, Justin, Elisabeth, and Charlize who are the loves of my life. I work hard so that you can be proud of who your mommy is, and so I can instill in you good habits for life. You know and see what it means to work hard and endure life's struggles. As an entrepreneur, no one can better understand the trials and the magnitude of sacrifice to raise children while running the business. You each are the joys of my life. Justin, my son, I am proud of you for doing your best as a dad for your son. My grandson David, I love you and pray for God to protect you every step of the way. I wish that I could be that Grandma that gets to love on you and hold you every day, but life just doesn't let us have it all.

My Lizzie, you are my special baby that will never know what it is like to be an adult. Although you are 24 years old, life gave mommy lemons, and I turned it to lemonade. I couldn't be a better mom without you, because you have taught me what it means to love unconditionally. My baby girl Charlize, you are a special gift from God, he blessed you with so much love and wisdom at your age. You acknowledge who you are, and why you were placed in this family, and that is to connect with others. You are such a great baby sister to your brother, and especially for Lizzie. You have helped her so much. You make mommy's life complete. I know I am hard on you at times, but it is because I don't want you to make the same mistakes that I did in life. I trust that God gives you wisdom and that I am a guard rail for your life. I love you all so very much with all my heart.

To Sopheak aka (Soup), my only brother, who I grew up with. Do you have any idea how very proud I am of you for being the person you are? Through all the tribulations you turned out ok! You have a great family of your own, are married to the amazing Trish, and have my cutest nephew, Kai Kai. To my twin sisters, Sophorn and Sophea aka Pia, you both made my life worth living through and under the Mango Tree. I am very proud of you both, for your own individual successes, and that you married great guys, John and Dan. Pia, I am proud of you for being a great mom to Lekhy.

Last, but certainly not least, my baby sister Sopha aka Daisy. I am the proudest older sister. I am proud of you for raising four amazing children --- Abigail, Isabel, Arya, and Solomon on your own most of the time while your awesome military husband Samuel, who is away much of the time serving overseas, protecting the United States. Samuel is such a great provider for Daisy. I love you all so very much for being who you are and being my sisters, and brother, nieces and nephews, and in--laws.

To Mark Matson, for being a coach to Charles. He has become a better financial coach, and that ripple effect continues out to millions of others. I am so blessed to have you as my coach as well. I wouldn't be able to finish this book successfully without people like you in my life.

To Xuan and Hoa Nguyen who were an inspiration in my life from the beginning of my journey in the Financial Services Industry. You both have been great role models and coaches. We have not worked together or spoken in over ten years, but your impact is still felt today. I would not be the person I am today without your influence in my life. I will be forever grateful.

To Mr. Bill Hawkins, you are such an amazing man of God, you loved and served the Khmer people in the same way that Christ loves us. Although I have not seen you for over twenty years, I am grateful that I had you in my early childhood. At the time, when you were trying to teach me the Bible, I did not understand what you were teaching. It is because of the seed you installed in me, that I have grown to love Christ. I chose Christ because of people like you who love Christ and show Christ's love through your actions. Christ was there all along he didn't let me go too far. I appreciate you for being the light in my life. You are a true servant of God. I am blessed to have you in my life.

To Ms. Jan Jacob, you gave me the best gift of all, "The Bible". That was the beginning of my true walk with Christ. Since that day when I first opened the BIBLE, God's words have been leading me every day. Thank you. I am forever grateful for your love and kindness to me when I was lost. You were the person who helped me to see the light. Thank you.

To all my friends, and everyone I encounter in daily life, each one of you has impacted me directly or indirectly in wonderful ways. I've learned what to do and what not to do from each encounter, and I thank you all that God placed you in my life.

Foreword

by Heidi Becicka

God has an amazing way of putting people together, and of ensuring that the paths of certain individuals cross at exactly the right time. While I am in my late 40's and have always grown up "Christian," my true walk of faith really only began a few short years back. I knew of God, but I didn't really know God, and I certainly didn't have a real relationship with Him. I thought I loved God and that He loved me, but I didn't really know how to lean into that and experience it fully. I had seen and even acknowledged what I thought was God's hand working in my life, but I still struggled with the uncertainties and doubts of my belief in this omnipotent God. Little did I know that God was right there with me, listening, and preparing just the right person to help move me forward in my faith walk.

In April of 2017, only a few weeks after moving completely across the country for my husband's new job, I attended a Bible study with about 300 women. It was on that beautiful morning that God led me to one of His most passionate followers, Sophal Pettit. Her love for Jesus and her desire to follow him faithfully just oozed out of her. It was not only inspiring but infectious.

It was about two months into our friendship that Sophal shared with me her extraordinary story of survival in the Killing Fields of Cambodia. Her stories continued with her family coming to America, struggling to assimilate to our culture, and working tirelessly to make it in their new country. For being as young as she is, Sophal has lived a lifetime of struggles and hardships. While these experiences have certainly impacted her, Sophal has not let them define her in any way. Sophal is a strong woman of God --- He is her identity, and she is the first to identify Him in every single one of these trials and triumphs.

It not only has been an honor to get to know Sophal and her story, but it has been life-changing for me, spiritually. It is impossible to listen to Sophal's stories and not see God's hand working, from the biggest to the simplest of things. She is an obedient follower of God, despite the circumstances, and when all is said and done, Sophal gives every bit of glory back to our loving God.

She has taught me what it's like to have unshakeable faith and pure joy in all circumstances. She has taught me that God is always with us, even in our struggles, and will grow us in His ways if we only let Him. She has taught me that prayer is key to our relationship with God --- talk to Him anywhere, and at all times. And lastly, she has taught me the importance of being obedient to God in everything that we do, because he loves us and has a purpose for our lives.

My prayer for this book is that God will use Sophal's story to strengthen the faith of all who read it, just like Sophal has done for me. Faith in God, faith in love, and faith in prayer.

Foreword

by Dinh Luong

You hold in your hands a piece of hidden treasure from the very heart of God. A true story of His amazing Grace, Love and Victory through my beloved sister-in-Christ, Sophal Pettit. She is one of the most caring, loving and generous people I know.

She is so passionate about sharing the love of Christ and helping others grow in the wisdom and knowledge of Him. I am truly blessed, grateful and honored to call her my friend and sister. Thank you, Sophal, for your ongoing love, encouragement, and support. Praise the Lord for our divine appointment.

As I am writing the Lord lead me to Isaiah 43:1- 4, "*But now, thus says the Lord, who created you, O Jacob, And He who formed you, O Israel: "Fear not, for I have redeemed you; I have called you by your name; You are Mine. When you pass through the waters, I will be with you; And through the rivers, they shall not overflow you. When you walk through the fire, you shall not be burned, Nor shall the flame scorch you. For I am the Lord your God, The Holy One of Israel, your Savior; I gave Egypt for your ransom, Ethiopia, and Seba in your place. Since you were precious in My sight, you have been honored, and I have loved you; Therefore, I will give men for you, and people for your life.*"

The living testimony of Sophal and her family is a true

3

reflection of God's promise and faithfulness. He was with them through all the trials and tribulations and called them by name because they are His from the very beginning. Facing death and hardship in the wilderness, they became overcomers and more than conquerors by the power of the living God who miraculously rescued them out of every dangerous situation.

May the blessing of God's hope, peace and strength be upon you as you read this heartfelt journey of triumph. And may God's light through Sophal overflow you with His perfect love and faith through Christ Jesus.

Foreword

By Charles Pettit

Sophal Pettit is affectionately known to me as "My Cambodian Princess". In February of 1997 I first laid my eyes on this amazing woman and I knew instantly that she was my soul mate.

I remember very shortly after we first met at a seminar, I conducted on Financial Planning my business partner Vincent Del Franco who is from Arizona came to visit me in Maryland. We drove to Pennsylvania to do some training for our new agent's joining our firm and Sophal was there that night. On our drive home I remember saying to Vincent totally out of the blue "I am going to marry that girl"! He looked at me as if he thought that I had lost my mind. A few months later our company had our annual award trip in Hawaii and when I showed up there with Sophal he could not believe it.

Within a year of that trip, Sophal became my wife. We married on October 10th,1998. This was the best personal decision I have ever made. Not only do we share a passion for each other but also for the entrepreneurial spirit. From that day on we decided to build our family and our future business together. Over the first ten years of our marriage we worked hard and built our family and business to a phenomenal success.

From 1998 to 2008 we worked extremely hard and had an incredible journey. During this time, we received many awards and recognitions. We topped all the charts which culminated in being named Executive Marketing Director --- MVP of The Year out of more than 25,000 independent producers in August of 2006 and Promoted to one of the highest Executive Field Leadership positions in the company as a CEO Marketing Director in January of 2007.

As CEO of our "company within the company" we felt an amazing sense of accomplishment as this was a goal, we set in 1998 and together worked very hard, stayed focused and made incredible sacrifices to achieve. During this ten-year period, we also enjoyed traveling around the world and had the opportunity to meet many amazing people that have impacted our lives in many ways.

Our travel destinations included repeated trips to Hawaii, and Europe, (Germany, Austria, Italy, Monte Carlo, The Greek Islands, Greece, France, and Croatia). Other world destinations included St. Martin, Tahiti, Philippines, Taiwan, and Mexico. We also met bestselling authors like Dr. Stephen R. Covey, Tom Peters, Harry S. Dent Jr., William E. Donoghue, & Ben Baldwin. Professional athletes like: Nascar driver, Carl Edwards, Quarter Back, Joe Namath, Boxing Great, Muhammad Ali, and Gold Medal Hockey Player Jim Craig. Particularly important to us was meeting great leaders like: Gen. H. Norman Schwarzkopf, Gen. Tommy R. Franks, and Coach Lou Holtz. We both agree that no-one had more impact on us and our success in business than our mentor in the firm, Mr. Xuan Nguyen.

Sophal Pettit is the heart and soul of the success we have had. Sophal has been the perfect wife and partner for a dreame like me. Many people have heroes in Sports figures or Movie Stars but for me, she is my Hero! She has such a wonderful spirit about her. People like to be around me more when she is there because she brings me to life. I am always trying to impress her. Sophal has always been there with me, in fact she has introduced me to most of our clients and most of the agents we have trained in the business over the years. I often joke and say, "She brings them to church, and I baptize them."

Couple power is the greatest power you can have in business. When Sophal told me that she had a dream to write her story in a book I jumped onboard right away because I know Sophal's personal story is very powerful and shows why she has always been destined for success. When she told me that her title was going to be "From Hell to Heaven", "From Surviving the Killing Fields in Cambodia to the Beatitudes of Living in Gratitude" I was very excited and have been her number one fan!

I must admit that prior to meeting my Wife in 1997 I had never even heard of the Country of Cambodia. As I learned more about her and her story I was totally blown away and had a deep sense of how fortunate I am to have been born and raised in America. As I investigated more about her and the Country, she was born in I discovered that she was born in Takeo, Cambodia, a small town near the Vietnamese border on July 16th, 1970.

The oldest of five children. At the very young age of fourteen, she arrived in the United States as a refugee. The first five years of her life would be considered normal for a young girl born in a third world country. Little did she know how much her life would change before she would ever be able to start something as basic as school. On April 17th, 1975 the Khmer Rouge, a communist guerrilla group led by Pol Pot, took power in Phnom Penh, the capital of Cambodia. They forced all city dwellers into the countryside and into labor camps.

During their rule, it is estimated that nearly 2 million Cambodians died by starvation, torture or execution. The Khmer Rouge turned Cambodia to "year zero". They banned all institutions, including stores, banks, hospitals, schools, religion, and the family. Everyone was forced to work 12 --- 14 hours a day, every day. Children were separated from their parents to work in mobile groups or as soldiers. People were fed one watery bowl of soup with a few grains of rice thrown in. Babies, children, adults and the elderly were frequently killed.

The Khmer Rouge killed people if they didn't like them, if they didn't work hard enough, if they were educated, if they came from different ethnic groups, or if they showed sympathy when their family members were taken away to be killed. All were killed without reason. Everyone had to pledge total allegiance to Angka, the Khmer Rouge government.

It was a campaign based on instilling constant fear and keeping their victims off balance. After the Vietnamese invaded and liberated the Cambodian people from the Khmer Rouge, 600,000 Cambodians fled to Thai border camps. Ten million landmines were left in the ground, one for every person in Cambodia. After Sophal and her family endured the unbearable conditions of the Pol Pot for four years they were finally able to escape towards Thailand in 1979. It took them until 1980 to make it to the Thailand border as they had to walk and avoid landmines along the route. They finally were taken by the United Nations to the Thailand Refugee camp.

Sophal says that when they arrived at the refugee camp her Mom applied to go to France and America. They agreed that whatever country accepted them first they would go to make a new life. A few years went by, and finally, they got accepted to come to America. That day was the happiest day in her life because America sounded like Heaven to her. Her mom told her that America was very clean, peaceful and that the people were very nice "just like heaven". Before they came to America, they had to pass all the government-issued tests. The family stayed in several camps in Thailand and the Philippines before they made it to America. They first arrived in the state of California. At that time Sophal was only fourteen. Her family could either choose to come to Pennsylvania or stay in California. Her parents chose to come to Pennsylvania. Sophal says "We finally felt safe and clean. There was good food on clean plates and clean silverware for us. There was shampoo and soap to shower in a clean bathroom". She had finally reached her "heaven".

Today Sophal thanks God daily for her and her family's life. Once arriving to the sweetest place on earth, Hershey, Pennsylvania, Sophal took on the next challenge to learn the English language and start school as a teenager in America. She successfully endured those difficult years and graduated from High School in 1990. Not being satisfied with the J•O•B mentality she started to look for ways to improve her life. She quickly realized that she needed to own her own business. After attempting several different businesses, she was introduced to me and the Financial Services Industry in February of 1997.

Sophal often says..."The difference between great people and everyone else is that great people create their lives actively, while everyone else is created by their lives, passively waiting to see where life takes them next. The difference between the two is the difference between living fully and just existing. Sophal and I oversee our future and we live fully." I am so proud of her and the power that she possesses.

The reason Sophal is so driven and works so hard is that she wants to take full advantage of the American Dream that she feels so blessed to be a part of. We are both very grateful for the opportunities that we have had and are very blessed with a wonderful family that has always been involved in the business. Today our two girls Elisabeth and Charlize help in the office and we look forward to teaching them the business and what it takes to work hard and achieve their goals. On our way to becoming a CEO, Sophal and I built a great distribution team which, at its peak, had trained more than 5,000 associates into mastering the Financial Services industry.

When the company went through many leadership and corporate changes, we realized that it could no longer take us where we wanted to go nor provide the opportunity for others that they had enjoyed. On December 31st, 2007, we resigned our position as CEO Marketing Director, ending our distinguished career. We knew it was time for a change.

This was not the first time we were faced with making a major decision and it was not an easy choice. We had accomplished quite a lot with the previous company and had been recognized for our achievements. We knew that there would be people who wouldn't understand why we would walk away from what many were still trying to achieve.

Sophal and I agreed that if we had to lose everything and start all over it would be worth it to build the company we wanted to build. Having faith in each other and our abilities to overcome whatever hardships might come, we looked forward not backward and saw a whole new future.

On January 1st, 2008 we launched our final chapter and decided to take our future into our own hands by growing our own Independent financial planning practice. For more than twenty years now we have helped thousands of families across this great nation achieve financial success through assisting them to get a comprehensive understanding of how to make their money work for them and then implementing plans to realize their dreams. We have set in motion an extraordinary system to shape the destiny of millions. The Lord has blessed us, and he continues to guide us. Sophal says. "I think he gave us everything we have for a good reason..., for stewardship. We will be good stewards of this company. We have to do right by people." Our goal is to spend the next thirty to forty years building this great company applying the Beatitudes of Living in Gratitude!

Enjoy this powerful story of an amazing woman that is not only a Survivor but a Thriver! She is my Cambodian Princess and I am so proud of her and her accomplishment. I believe one of the hardest things there is to do is to write a book. You did it, Honey! May God continue to bless you!

Love, Your Husband, and Soul Mate

Charles Pettit

Introduction

As I begin my story, I've decided to add the background of the life I lived during my childhood. It will provide a frame of reference that will connect you to the stories I will tell throughout this book.

The Cambodian Genocide

The Khmer Rouge took control of the Cambodian government in 1975, with the goal of turning the country into a communist agrarian utopia. In reality, they emptied the cities and evacuated millions of people to labor camps where they were starved and abused.

Doctors, teachers and other educated people, as well as monks, the rich, and anyone perceived to be in opposition, was tortured and killed.

It is estimated that between 1.7 and 2 million Cambodians died during the 4-year reign of the Khmer Rouge, with little to no outcry from the international community.

On April 17, 1975, the Khmer Rouge seized control of the country's capital city, Phnom Penh, effectively ousting the Lon Nol government. They immediately began emptying the city's population into labor camps in the countryside, where physical abuse, disease, exhaustion, and starvation were extremely prevalent.

Their policies were radical adaptations of Maoist and Marxist-

Leninist theories, attempting to transform Cambodia into a rural, classless society comprised of collectivized farms. The country's name was changed to Democratic Kampuchea in 1976 and Pol Pot declared it "Year Zero" as he began building his new republic.

In the beginning, executions were not necessary – starvation served as an effective tool to dispose of undesirable populations, but as more and more people were sent to prison, the Khmer Rouge moved over to a system of "killing fields," establishing hundreds all over Cambodia.

As the genocide progressed, survival was determined by one's ability to do work on the collective farms. This meant many of Cambodia's elderly, handicapped, ill, and children became targets due to their inability to undertake harsh manual labor. Money, free markets, schools, private property, foreign styles of clothing, religious practices, and other aspects of traditional Khmer culture were abolished, and buildings such as schools, pagodas, and in the beginning, executions were not necessary – starvation served as an effective tool to dispose of undesirable populations, but as more and more people were sent to prison, the Khmer Rouge moved over to a system of "killing fields," establishing hundreds all over Cambodia.

As the genocide progressed, survival was determined by one's ability to do work on the collective farms. This meant many of Cambodia's elderly, handicapped, ill, and children became targets due to their inability to undertake harsh manual labor.

Money, free markets, schools, private property, foreign styles of clothing, religious practices, and other aspects of traditional

Khmer culture was abolished, and buildings such as schools, pagodas, and government properties were turned into prisons, stables, camps, and granaries. Family relationships were heavily criticized, and the Khmer Rouge insisted that everyone consider "Angka" (translated to the Organization, referring to the top level of the regime) as their mother and father. Child soldiers were a huge tool of the Khmer Rouge, as they were easy to control and would follow orders without hesitation, to the point where many were forced to shoot their own parents.

The killing fields were sites set up all over the country where the Khmer Rouge took people to be killed once they could no longer work, had "confessed" to their alleged crimes, or simply just were not seen as being useful anymore. It is estimated that over one million people were killed at these sites and were buried in mass graves.

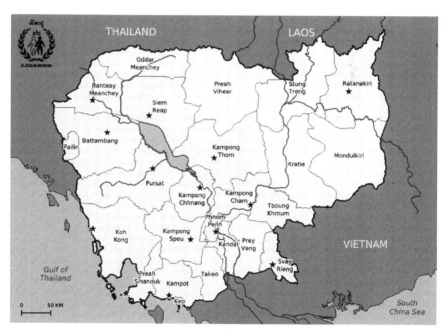

Cambodia

Today, many of the killing fields have been excavated to give the victims a proper burial but some are also inaccessible due to landmines. One of the more famous ones is Choeung Ek located on the outskirts of Phnom Penh. Here people were taken for execution after enduring torture and interrogation at the S-21 prison, a former high school. It has been turned into a memorial site for visitors to learn about the genocide and pay their respects to the victims.

Life after the Khmer Rouge

Rebuilding the country was extremely difficult as there was little foreign aid and all existing infrastructure had been destroyed by Pol Pot's regime. For a long time, the country did not have any doctors, teachers, engineers, or other professionals because they had all been executed.

PTSD was very prevalent among survivors, though it largely went untreated throughout the 1990s due to the lack of healthcare professionals in the country, as well as a tradition of silence surrounding the atrocities. The level of destruction inflicted by the Khmer Rouge has greatly contributed to the large amounts of poverty that many Cambodians face today.

Cambodia today is still in a state of recovery from the atrocities committed by the Khmer Rouge. The country is laden with millions of landmines, which have contributed to more deaths and disabilities even up to the present. It is estimated that roughly 40,000 people in Cambodia are amputees due to landmines. Many families separated during the period of the regime still have not reunited.

Though the Khmer Rouge no longer exists, many participants in Cambodian politics were previously influential members of the organization. This includes Prime Minister Hun Sen, a former Khmer Rouge battalion commander. There are also former members living in the countryside; in many villages, people have lived side by side with them for decades.

This article can be referenced at http://endgenocide.org/learn/past-genocides/the-cambodian-genocide/

The website is called: United to End Genocide.

-1-

Stories from My Childhood

By Pia Garonzi

I often wondered what it was like to experience severe hunger, to be confronted with imminent death all around, see families ripped apart, and be forced to grow up fast. The little girl who was forced to grow up fast is my older sister, Sophal. The world may know her as an outspoken wife to Charles Pettit, a mother of three children, a Christian Cambodian, but in our family, she is affectionately known as our, "Bong Srey" (*eldest girl*).

Sophal is the eldest sister of our tight-knit family of seven that includes my parents, older brother Sopheak (aka Soup), my twin sister Sophorn, and baby sister, Sopha (aka Daisy). I am one of the twins, a middle child of our family. By 1979, my twin and I were born and by that time, the civil war in Cambodia ceased. Our family trekked by foot towards the border of Thailand to resettle in the refugee camps and eventually made our way here to America, arriving during the cold of winter, enduring the frigid temperatures of January 1984. Because my twin sister Sophorn and I were born post-war, we have no tangible memories of what life was like in Cambodia. The memories are sketchy, so I only remember the refugee camp in the Philippines. Walking barefoot to preschool with my twin sister, and the sweet taste of dried powder milk were the only things left in my mind's memory bank of our time in a refugee camp.

From Hell to Heaven

Like so many Cambodian children that either grew up or were born in the late 1970s, Sophal had vivid and recurring memories of a time when it was all about surviving and making sure their loved ones were safe and together. I can boldly say, that Sophal was quick-witted and fiercely brave from having gone through those experiences. She was forced to learn the skills necessary, like foraging for food, trading goods for food, cooking, cleaning and caring for her younger siblings and parents for survival postwar. Most Cambodian children that experienced the horrors and hardships of the Khmer Rouge era had their innocent worlds destroyed, shaken and turned upside down. Indeed, this was considered the most turbulent and destructive time in Cambodia's history.

We grew up in a small town in central Pennsylvania and our family slowly assimilated into American life and culture. Like other immigrant families, we struggled in many ways to assimilate and adjust to our new lives. My parents, especially, desperately clung onto our culture and language; and fortunately, found other Cambodian families that resettled in the area. Even now, if I smell a whiff of incense, it takes me back to my childhood where, in my family's living room, the incense would be placed next to the neatly adorned variety of fruits, rice buns wrapped in grape leaves, and other Khmer food. Below these items and at the center of it all, hung pictures of the grandparents I never got to meet. I never understood why we were not allowed to eat the food placed on the altar, and why the "spirits" of our ancestors got to enjoy all this delicious food meticulously placed there in the family's living room, where it sat for days. Now, I fully understand why my parents held on so tightly to what they knew and practiced in Cambodia.

While the rest of America was experiencing the AIDS crisis, the Reagan era and MTV was the hip new channel on TV, we struggled with intense hatred and racism toward us while living in our small town. My siblings can attest to the endless amounts of racial slurs directed at them while at school from the American kids making fun of us and telling us to, "*get back on the boat, and go back to where you came from.*"

I remember being so afraid when, in the middle of the night, a group of "*saw*" (white-colored kids) decided to communicate their hatred of us by throwing tomatoes at our house. These smashed up tomatoes were everywhere – on our front porch and door, and broke one of our living room windows. The racism continued when, in junior high school, there was a kid named, Michael Jackson (yes, a *saw* tall, scrawny kid with the exact same name as the pop icon).

I remember harboring feelings of hate towards this kid whenever I saw him in the hallway after he had badgered us by saying, "*ching-chong, ching-chong.*" I never knew whatever happened to him, but his name and the hatred associated with his name still resonated in me. Experiences like these, I believe, have made my family stronger. As much as they had endured the pain and sufferings of the Pol Pot regime, this seemed like an easier obstacle to hurdle over – the lesser of the two evils. The hatred we experienced as a family has spurred us on to love our neighbors even more.

Every day, I see my family love people more, and generously give more to people they do not know. We could live a life of bitterness, holding a grudge against those that did us wrong, or be resentful, but we chose not to take that path. It may sound cliché, but my family continues to choose to live in peace and love. Because my parents and older siblings have experienced near death, along with the hatred and the struggles of being refugees, they have chosen to live their lives with a deep sense of gratitude for the life God has given to them.

Even though we grew up together under the same roof, our lives were a huge contrast in some ways. In hindsight, the stark contrasts of our lives were a blessing in disguise. That is where, I have learned tough love and resilience; and drew much strength from Sophal's life experiences. My parents, like most families in the Asian cultures, held the eldest child to higher expectations and regarded them to be the most responsible, dependable and trustworthy.

Indeed, our "Bong Srey" truly lived up to these high standards and has not failed to meet the expectations of what the oldest child should be. Because my older sister was supposed to be the "responsible one," my mom and Sophal shared their versions of a story of when being the oldest has its consequences. The "la-khown" (musical theater with comedy acts) was in town and Sophal really wanted to attend the show. Instead of going by herself, she decided to take me along. I was a toddler who, Sophal described as, "stuck to my hip." Everywhere we went, I wouldn't walk, but was always carried around with my legs wrapped around either my brother or Sophal's hips.

Sometime during the show, someone in the audience threw something hard like a rock, and it hit my little head. Thankfully, I wasn't hospitalized, but upon our arrival home, my parents were supremely angry and Sophal was physically punished by our father. In her young mind, she could have not anticipated the dangerous risk to herself nor her younger sister but was only a little girl who enjoyed and loved seeing the *la-khown* come to town.

Growing up, my parents worked a lot so there were many fond memories of Sophal and Soup "raising" us – taking on not only the parental duties such as, supervising us, disciplining and making sure we were dressed and ready for school, but they helped my parents tremendously with translating and working several odd jobs like picking blueberries in New Jersey during the summer months. As a teenager, not only did she have to balance going to school, a job and looking after her younger siblings, but the wages that Sophal earned from work, she willingly gave to my parents. She was a hard worker and all that she earned assisted my parents financially.

When I was in elementary school, I remember learning about the Christmas Holiday. Christmas has become one of my all-time favorite holidays. Even now, I am still in awe of this time of year when all around you, houses in town were beautifully lit up, there were images of neatly wrapped presents under the trees, the churches displayed their best manger scene and Santa popped up at the malls. I remember one of the Christmases when Sophal worked at the local Kmart. Truly, it was a special Christmas memory for me, because we received brand-new pink dresses from Sophal!

At that time, my mom, a master seamstress, made dresses and other clothes for our family. If we wanted a new dress or needed clothes for school, we made many field trips to the West Shore Evangelical Free Church for used clothes. Needless to say, these new pink dresses were pretty darn special for the three of us! It was also exciting because we received these dresses as Christmas gifts.

These ruffled pretty pink dresses with the white laces on the front chest fitted perfectly on our petite under-nourished framed bodies. Along with the pretty pink dresses were purses, white pantyhose tights and black dress shoes for the three of us. These dresses made us look like triplets and I thought this gift was the most wonderful Christmas gift from my older sister. We proudly wore our pink dresses as much as we could. We wore them to birthday parties, Cambodian New Year's, and even posed in them for one of our family portraits. All I remember thinking was, "How lucky I am to have an older sister that bought us a new dress for Christmas."

I cannot even begin to fathom the pain and suffering my sister experienced as a child. Where I played on the nicely cut green grasses and roamed freely on the playgrounds and streets of Hummelstown, my older sister had to either work or had to "babysit" her three younger siblings. Even though our lives were carved out in different directions, we both ended up believing and following our Lord and Savior, Jesus Christ. I am grateful for an older sister – who, unfortunately, experienced and endured hardships in contrast to my childhood experiences. But through her tough experiences, I found that there are teachable moments that she has passed down to the next generation that will only ever read the horrific stories of the Khmer Rouge online and what they did to scar a generation of their own people.

This is not just another "feel good" story of a survivor but of a journey (one that she is still walking on) of strength, wit, and resilience that has inspired my family and others that have met my older sister. We can certainly try our best to empathize and sympathize, but we will never know what it was like. I, along with everyone else, is someone peering into her life with glass spectacles looking from the outside into the heart of a courageous woman of God.

My sister's journey is someone who now faithfully walks with God; entrusting her every breath of life in her Lord and Savior. In God, she chooses joy, healing and a living hope to her loved ones and to a broken world that is in desperate need of hope and peace. Fortunately, her story of her journey en-route to heaven – the final destination – does not end in darkness, death, and despair but it is a journey of healing from the past, a light shining brightly to a fallen world and a living hope for the future. Moreover, a living hope that is only found when one chooses the path of courage, of healing, forgiveness, and finding strength each day in her True Maker, the giver of life, love and hope – that is, Jesus Christ. I not only can proclaim and proudly boast that we share our genetic makeup and that of our namesake and that she is my one and only, "bong srey," but a sister in Christ as well.

I hope her stories provoke you to dream big, and that each word compels you to live a life that is bigger than yourselves as you will be immersed in all the humor, the heart-warming tales; and traumatic stories that will tug and tear at your heart as to draw you closer each day to a loving and faithful God.

-2-

My Early Childhood

I was born in Takeo, Cambodia, a small town near Vietnam. My family name is Choup. I am the oldest child in my family of seven. Life, before 1975 was beautiful to me. I loved being spoiled by my aunts and uncles. I had all the toys I wanted. I had dozens of pairs of shoes in many different colors and remember being fascinated with elevators. My curious little mind thought they were magic, as I watched people step inside, then disappear right in front of me.

My mom was born into a farming family in 1944. Their business was growing rice. Her family spoke Chinese, Vietnamese, and Cambodian (Khmer). Growing up, she was not interested in learning Chinese, because she felt like the letters looked like crabs crawling around.

She was the only one in her family that had gone to a university and was a teacher before she met my dad, substitute teaching for all grade levels. She stopped teaching after she met my dad so she could help him run his café. They sold noodle and rice soups, and baked goods. While most girls were taught homemaking skills such as cooking and sewing, she did not learn to cook until my dad taught her. My father always joked that her cooking would kill people! In time, she became a better cook than my dad.

My dad was born into a farming/fishing family in 1942. His mom died when he was only seven days old, and he ended up

27

being passed back and forth between family members. He did not get an education and so, did not have status in the community. He was, however, a hard worker and an honest man.

Every morning, my dad would put me on his shoulders, and walk to the restaurant he owned, then treat me to his freshly baked French bread and coffee with condensed milk, (French café latte). I loved those mornings with him! I still remember the amazing smell.

After breakfast, my dad would let me play with the other children in the marketplace. I developed a knack for stealing the bags and baskets of the shoppers. My mom would gather them up and return them. Thank goodness for their honesty!

In 1975, everything changed. The Khmer Rouge overturned the Cambodian government. The guerrilla army, led by an insanely oppressive leader named Pol Pot, quickly wreaked havoc on the people of our country. Our family was no exception. I was only five years old when the communists reached our home in Phnom Penh, Cambodia's capital.

Brainwashed Cambodian soldiers following Pol Pot's orders destroyed many buildings in the city. They began killing the high-ranking military families as well as families with wealth and/or education who had Chinese or Vietnamese bloodlines. My mother was highly educated and saw this coming, so we escaped to a village in the jungle far away from the city, leaving behind family, homes, belongings, and businesses.

Before the war, we were living in a beautiful home. We had

clean water to drink and modern conveniences. Overnight, it turned to hell. Luckily, we ended up in a small village where no one knew of our background. We lived in a tiny hut with a dirt floor, and with no clean water. Our water system was the rain, which is the only way we could drink and bathe. Food was scarce. Our bathroom was on the jungle floor, which was occupied by snakes and other creatures. Our toilet paper was leaves. We quickly learned to pick the right kind of leaves, as the wrong ones would leave us burning and itching for days. They made us dye what we had left of our colorful clothing black, and no shoes just our bare feet. Slowly our belongings disappeared.

My parents were forced to work in the rice fields and to do all the farming for the Khmer Rouge (Pol Pot) as well as build the road for them to walk on. My brother and I were forced to watch the cows and buffalo in order to receive any food for lunch or dinner. Our typical food of the day was rice soup.

Not long after that, my parents were taken away. My little brother and I ended up taking care of each other. We lived in a shack, built by bamboo sticks and hay. We survived on a few pieces of rice and unclean water each day. Life was pure hell and full of evil. At ages four and seven, my brother and I waited day in and day out for our parents to return. After several months went by, my brother got very sick; his body looked like a skeleton. His skin was very pale, and his stomach was very large. His testicles were glowing like a light bulb. His eyes were deep as a well. I thought he would not survive due to a lack of nutrition.

Days turned to months, and months turned to years. Each day, the two of us worked for an insane army in return for a tiny portion of watered-down rice soup. We were starving to death and began looking like skeletons. For food, I searched for anything edible. We ate tiny ants, grasshoppers, and any other kind of creatures we could find. At one point, I was so hungry; I ate cow skin. To quench our thirst, we drank unclean water from a small pond that was polluted with human and animal waste. Our stomachs grew like watermelons. Our skin had dark spots, and our bodies had a yellow color. We had only one pair of clothes that we wore to work and to sleep.

To be clean, we showered in the rain and dried off by running around in the sun. I got the chickenpox, and there was no medicine and no parents to comfort me. We both had many infections on our bodies from the jungle bugs and lack of nutrition. 1975-1978 were the most horrific years, and I remember waiting to die but wanting to live.

I learned how to be still. At night I would sneak into the rice fields and steal rice to feed my brother and me. I was tiny and quick. I'd crawl in the dark field and picked the rice and put it in my bag. I could hear the sound of wind and small creatures, but it did not scare me away.

Thank God, I never ran into poison snakes while I was running around the jungle and the rice fields. When the bag was full, I would crawl out of the field and run as fast as I could.

My brother and I had no education. We did not know what day or time it was, only how to live and how to survive. We were not allowed to go to school. Later in life, I learned that for Pol Pot to control the people, he would not allow children to be educated, and they killed many of the educators.

People around us died one after another. They were either killed by Pol Pot's army or by starvation. Pol Pot and his army controlled our lives and everything we owned.

Eventually, my parents returned to visit us for a couple of days. They broke down and cried when they saw us because we were so skinny. We all cried without teardrops. We all were hurting inside out. Like us, they looked like walking skeletons.

The worst part was in 1978. It was close to the time when the Vietnamese took over my country. My father got very sick, and we thought he died. My mom gathered help and was about to bury him. As we began to wrap him for burial, my mom decided to check him one more time. Suddenly he started breathing and came back to life. We hurriedly gave him some rice soup so he could get his energy back. Later, when he got better, he told us that when he passed, he went to a place where they opened a 'big name book', asked him his name, and when he told them, his name was not in the book.

Then my mom got very ill. She was taken to this horrible "hospital." (To me it looked like a death field, "The Walking Dead.") The hospital was littered with dead bodies. There was no bathroom. Nobody had shoes to wear. Everywhere you went, you would step on human waste. The place was hell. The whole country was hell. We were living in hell.

Every day I had to walk a long way to bring food to my mom. The food I brought her was nothing more than a few pieces of rice filled with water, and whatever scraps I could find, but it gave me a reason to see my mom. I never wanted my parents to leave me. Today, I can't even imagine my children or nieces or nephews, at that age going through what I have gone through.

I lived to tell you my story.

One day, on my way to the hospital of hell, to bring whatever little food I had found for her, I saw my "Loc Bras Ta" (My God Angel). It was getting dark, and the sound of the wind rubbed against the trees, scaring me. I was by myself. I looked around, but there was nobody there. I was in the middle of the jungle, crossing from one field to another. Almost everywhere I turned, I saw dead people lying around like animals. There was no one around; I heard only the wind and small creatures. Suddenly, I saw an old man dressed in white cloth. He was sitting on a log. Then I stopped feeling afraid. I went and stood beside him without saying a word or even looking at him. I never knew who he was, or if he existed at all. I told my parents about it, and they said he was my "Loc Bras Ta" (My God Angel).

I was about eight years old. People were dying daily from starvation.

Scared and worried, my parents sent me to live with a man that lived far away from them. He gave me food to eat, and a roof over my head. They thought it would be better for my life. I did have food to eat, but I was missing my family. I became very sick with a high fever and began hallucinating. I saw statues of lions that normally were in front of the temple. They ran after me and barked like wolves. I could not work, but I had to be around people so that I would not be afraid. I missed my family so much that I wanted to die. The man finally took me back to my parents and brother, understanding that I was dying from grief and loneliness.

In 1979 the Vietnamese took over my country, and my family

escaped. We ran toward Thailand's border, where we heard the United Nations could help us get to America. Our journey to Thailand's border was very long and exhausting. My father had gone to look for food for us but was captured and spent several months in jail with mountain soldiers. They imprisoned him because they thought that he was a spy for the Vietnamese soldiers. While my father was in jail, we had very little food and water.

My mom had just had my twin baby sisters, born under a Mango tree. We lived under that big Mango tree for quite some time. We didn't know if my father was dead or alive. My mom and I went begging for food. We were starving, and no one offered any food or water. At that point, I had no choice and began digging graves looking for gold jewelry to sell.

We even asked relatives for food, but, perhaps out of fear, they all turned their backs on us. They acted like they did not know us. Even when my mom offered to pay them back, they refused.

Finally, my father returned, and when he did, he brought with him a bag of food and goodies. At first, my mom was very upset wondering with questions why he left us for so long. He told her what had happened, and we all started to cry. We were just glad that he was alive.

My father sat us down and told us about what had happened to him for the three months he was away. After he was released from jail, he found a bag that he could use to carry items to sell to people so that he could make money to buy food for us. As it turned out, the bag he found belonged to a dead person who had been robbed on the road in the jungle. Jungle soldiers were looking for the bag and were trying to find the person who had killed the man that had that bag.

Knowing that being caught with the bag would mean certain death, my dad left the bag sitting on a tree. It was full of goodies that he had been trying to sell so that he could bring food to us. Now, he had to stay away from his family even longer to have the money. He traveled by foot to get to the border of Thailand and Cambodia. It was a long journey.

It was one of the saddest stories to hear from him. My dad never seemed to catch a break. When he was an infant, his mother died a week after he was born. His father could not afford to care for him, so he was passed from one stranger to another. He never got to attend school but worked for those families as a slave. One thing I can say for my dad is that he never had a "poor me" mentality. He was and is happy and grateful to be alive. He might not have the book smarts, but he surely has the street smarts with a good and wonderful heart. He loves to help people. (You got to make the best of your situation that you are put in, is what he always says.)

After my father returned, we made our way on foot, to Thailand. My parents each carried one of my twin sisters. We saw people blown up by land mines. At one point, we all had to cross a river. The water was at my parent's hips and reached just under my chin with my head raised high. We took turns carrying the twins, so my dad could carry some of our belongings above his head to not get them wet. I carried one of the twin sisters above my head walking through the water.

Bodies were everywhere, but we kept on moving until we reached the Thailand border.

We finally reached a Thailand Refugee Camp run by the United

Nations, called "Khao I Dang refugee camp 1980-1981." Many

people applied to go to America, France, Australia, and other countries. My mom applied to America and France; whichever country accepted us first that was where we would go.

While waiting at the Thailand camp to come to America, I learned how to read and write in our native language. I sold fruits to help my parents. I also babysat my sisters and cooked for them while my parents worked in the Thailand community.

A few years went by, and we got accepted to America. That day was the happiest day of our lives because America sounded like heaven to us. My mom told us that America was very clean, peaceful, and the people were very nice, just like heaven.

Before we came to America, we had to pass all the government regulations tests. We stayed in several different camps in Thailand and the Philippines before we left. In 1984, I arrived in America at the age of thirteen, along with my family of seven. Why, or how fate had allowed us to come this far is still a mystery to me. In my case, there were many times I could have been killed, but I think God was watching over me, he had a purpose and that purpose had yet to come.

There were sponsors for my family. We arrived in California, with the choice of staying in California or moving to

Pennsylvania. My parents chose to go to Pennsylvania.

We finally felt safe and clean. There was good food on clean plates and silverware. There were shampoo and soap, clean water to bathe in, and a clean bathroom. We had clean water to drink. Even though the clothing we received was used, it was the best we ever had. We had finally reached our heaven.

I thank God every day for my life and my family's lives.

Several years after we came to the United States, my parents received the news that all our relatives who went back to the hometown were killed and buried in a big pit, like the others. Some had been buried alive. Our tears still flow.

As you continue to read my story, I wish to share why I chose to name my book, "From Hell to Heaven," and the lessons I have learned that led me to live a life enjoying and appreciating the beatitudes of gratitude.

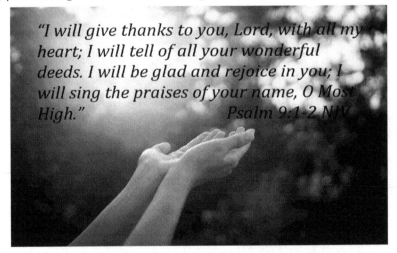

"I will give thanks to you, Lord, with all my heart; I will tell of all your wonderful deeds. I will be glad and rejoice in you; I will sing the praises of your name, O Most High."
Psalm 9:1-2 NIV

-3-

Hard Work

I was five-years-old when the chaos in Cambodia began. I feel that I never got to be a child. Now, I am almost fifty years old, and I just want to be a kid!

There was no choice but to work hard, it was a matter of life and death, and the fact that I did not die will forever feel like a miracle to me. Having worked in the killing fields of Cambodia tending the rice, and watching cows and buffalos, I was no stranger to working. In Cambodia, it meant work with no pay while nearly starving to death.

When we finally came to the United States of America, I worked in the blueberry fields, for pay!

I finally got a chance to go to school for the first time when I was fourteen years old. I was so excited that I woke up at midnight to get ready for school, and it felt like forever before the sun came up. I did not speak a word of English, and I had no understanding of the American culture. I was the only Asian kid in a classroom of white children. It was 1984 in the city of Hummelstown, Pennsylvania. I was so small; they put me in second grade for a few weeks, until they realized I was fourteen years old and moved me to sixth grade.

The kids in my classroom had never seen an Asian kid in person and quite likely had heard their parents talk about the

Vietnam war. They called me "Ching Chong, Ching Chong" and "gook." Fortunately, I did not understand what they were saying, but I knew I was completely different from everyone in my class!

It was a shock to me, and my struggles were real. I felt like I was deaf and dumb at the same time. That year I diligently worked to understand and speak English. I wanted so badly to fit in.

Understanding the value of hard work compensated for my language barriers, and having gone through the hell of Cambodia, nothing was going to stop me.

I live in a free country now, and though I babysat and picked blueberries all summer, rising at 5 AM to catch a bus to the fields, I was constantly working hard. I oversaw my four younger siblings while my parents worked. The younger ones were still under four years of age, and I was responsible for my brother, who was three years younger than me. Picking blueberries was not an easy job, but I found a way to pick quickly and fill more baskets every day. I focused on getting 50 trays a day because each tray I filled paid $2.50. This meant that if I could fill 50 trays, I made $125 a day. Meanwhile, this meant that I was three hours away from my siblings, who were being cared for by my brother and father.

I worked several other odd jobs and gave my parents everything that I earned. I became a young entrepreneur even when I was in the refugee camp. I found 10 "bat", (Thailand money) and turned it into hundreds more for my mom to buy whatever she needed. I sold fruits to travelers with the 10 bat I found, purchasing one pineapple that turned into many

pineapples I was able to sell. Between selling fruits and watching my little siblings, I had no time to play and yet, somehow, I found a way to have fun with kids around me.
Even though we lived in a small room with cockroaches and rats running around at night, it was still so much better than the life I had known before. I felt blessed. It was "My Heaven" to know that America was now myhome.

After three summers of picking blueberries, I was finally old enough to earn a paycheck legally. I worked part time at Wendy's, Weis Market, K·Mart, and Turkey Hill. During the summer I worked full time at the Hotel Hershey as a housekeeper. I then learned that I could earn more income as a Nursing Assistant which I also did during my high school years. I was willing to do things most kids my age was unwilling to do, such as cleaning up after the patient's bowel movements. It was a tough job, but it was much better than flipping burgers at Wendy's. I learned at a young age the value of life skills and taking care of people when they needed help the most.

After graduating from high school, I went directly to NEC Thompson Institute for two years and obtained my associate degree in Business Technology. After graduation, I got a job with Blue Cross Blue Shield and also worked as a manager for a small press company.

Meanwhile, my parents both worked multiple jobs from the moment they stepped foot in America. My dad worked at the Hershey Hotel and worked at a farm on his days off. He never took a day off in over twenty years. My mom worked as a seamstress during the day, and sewed at home during the evenings, for a company in Allentown, PA. We would drive to the factory in Allentown and pick up the pre-cut shirts and pants by the batch and would sew through the evening. We finally invested in a commercial sewing machine, and we did that work for many years.

Today, if I have nothing to do, I feel guilty. I am quite sure I will never retire. I love what I do as a mom, a grandma, and a business owner. Having come to this country with nothing, proved to be both a blessing and a curse. The blessing is that I found creative ways to make a living that many people of privilege would not do. I have life skills and experiences that will allow me to survive wherever I go and whatever happens. The curse was that I did not have any understanding of basic life skills and what it means to grow up in America. I feel that I made many mistakes.

When I was 18 years old, I met the man who would become my husband. We married and had two children together. The marriage was doomed from the beginning. I was young and inexperienced. I married the wrong person and married way too young to know it.

When I was four months pregnant with my daughter Elisabeth, he kicked me, in a fit of rage. Earlier that evening he was drinking at a bar uptown. I had driven to pick him up, and when I would not let him drive because he was so drunk, he refused to get in the car. I told him that it was fine, he could walk home, and I drove away.

When he arrived home, he grabbed me of the bed, kicking and pushing me down the stairs. Bruised and bleeding, I grabbed my son and drove all night, not knowing where to go. Finally, with guilt and shame, I showed up at my parents' home. The fighting and arguing happened regularly. We'd been kicked out of several apartments for disturbing the peace. All I wanted was to keep my children safe.

I left my ex-husband and my jobs in P because I could not handle the abuse. He once told me that if I left him, he would "do OJ" on me. OJ or not, I was so sick and tired of being sick and tired that I finally mustered up the courage to leave. I went to live in Annandale, VA. It took him over a year to find us. By then he was already involved with a younger girl, and they had moved into the house I had bought.

I fought for custody of my children, which resulted in a ten-year battle. Initially, the judge granted full custody to me, but then my ex filed for custody claiming I had kidnapped my children. He wanted me back. Fortunately, I had kept all the cards and letters he had written that were full of apologies. He sent flowers to my workplace as well. I kept those cards and letters, and they are what eventually helped me win full custody again.

There were times when both physically and mentally, I was a mess and was discouraged and exhausted. There were times I wanted to call it quits, but taking my life was not an option. It may have seemed like the solution at the time; it would be an easy way out, but not an option. My kids saved my life. I lived for them. The thought of leaving my kids with no mother was harder to bear. Since giving up was not an option, and I discovered in those times of darkness, that if I looked for things to do, like helping people, or putting more work on my plate, I would be so busy that I would not have time to think about my pain and could move past it.

Through my brokenness and suffering, God had a plan for me.

On February 13, 1997, I met Charles. He said it was love at first sight for him. Initially, I was clueless. I was working two jobs, living in a tiny apartment, sleeping on a comforter on the floor with my entire focus on making sure my children were safe and healthy. We lived near a school where I was able to find a babysitter that could walk my son to kindergarten.

When Charles moved in with me, he had only two black garbage bags filled with military clothing, two ugly sweaters, and two suits that were two sizes too big for him. He did not even have a suitcase.

We started from scratch. With nothing. Charles became my soul mate and my husband on October 10th, 1998. When life threw us lemons, we made lemonade! It was not easy at first, but together, we began building a business in the financial services industry, saving every penny to pay office rent. We lived on ramen noodles that cost five cents a pack.

At one point, we operated several businesses at the same time. We offered financial services including insurance, mortgage, and real estate. For thirteen long years, we worked hard day in and day out, but without God's foundation, it could not sustain us. We became the victims of our own success. We both only had 24 hours in a day, and we dedicated most of those hours to our business. So much so, that our kids want nothing to do with the business.

We found that because we didn't have the proper foundation and wisdom everything washed and blew away like building a house on sand. From this experience, we now know the difference because we have been there. I can share with my loved ones that they don't have to go through life the hard way.

We are now building a strong foundation on rocks for them from God's wisdom. All they must do is follow. Without God's wisdom, all we had was what we had learned from our parents and our worldly experiences. It was like working in the dark, not knowing what was right or wrong.

During our time in real estate, we spent three years as landlords. We had difficulty collecting money from our tenants because we gave people a chance after listening to their sob stories. I ended up disillusioned and was so ready to give up because I could not deal with other people's problems any longer. I was so naive and trusted people. I had inherited that trusting spirit from my parents as they to loved helping others, and often ended up being victims of their own kindness.

We worked so much that we missed our family birthday parties and graduations. We took no time off, and work was our only priority. Perhaps coming from an underprivileged background, I wanted so badly to win that I was willing to work longer and harder than anybody else. Though we made good money, we always put it back into our business. We built our dream home, then sold it to keep our business offices moving forward. I felt like the foundation around me was crumbling.

I recall a time when I was interviewing to recruit financial advisors to our company. A very sophisticated individual, who had an impressive background in financial services started asking so many questions of me that I finally deferred him to my husband. Because I did that, he told Charles that his secretary was very incompetent! Looking back, I can chuckle now, because at that moment I did not know what incompetent meant, so it did not bother me. When I DID find out what it meant, I felt so hurt and offended. Ignorance was bliss, but that bliss was short-lived! I have had to learn to not allow what others think of me to hurt me because it is not my business what others think of me. I did, however, learn from my lack of knowledge and have chosen to grow and improve.

In the summer of 2007, I called it quits! I was simply exhausted. I could not stand the model of the business; I could not stand dealing with the people. I no longer believed in the dream we were selling. I had become ill and had shingles all over my body and felt that no one knew or cared about me. At this point in my life, I had become a victim of my own choices.

Through that journey, my husband and I gained so many skills. Most certainly, we learned "what not to do." As the old saying goes the definition of insanity is continuing to do the same things you have always done and expecting different results.

My husband used to say that if you cut our wrists, we would bleed that company. I didn't want to compete with that.

I thought at that time, when I told him I was quitting the business, then for sure, he would divorce me. My mindset was to start over again. I didn't know how to say the words to him. How could I bring this conversation to his attention to tell him that I no longer wanted this business, and I want a divorce? That night I was traveling home, and I stopped on the I-95 crying my eyeballs out. I screamed out loud to the universe, saying that if there is a God out there, he'd better show me the way! I just felt so hopeless. We had worked so hard in our business that we had very little time if any for each other as husband and wife.

It seemed the harder we worked, the people around us got the best of us and we had nothing left to give to each other, nor to our children. I was struggling to make some sense out of my life. I felt like the harder I worked, the less I had. I was thinking to myself, "Dang I can't even afford a nice kitchen and I love to cook!" My kitchen had fallen apart and so did I! I had enough.

That summer of 2007, when I quit our business, I found myself. On that night driving down the I-95, a sense of peace came over me. I went home and waited for my husband to come home to tell him what was going on in my head. I was ready to tell him, "I quit, and I want a divorce." I did just that, and I almost died.

I began helping Charles in our financial business during the day while the kids were in school. Many of the agents that we had in our former financial business had joined us as we built a new business with a fresh and solid business model.

That July 2007, when I left the company, I also found myself, and I found God. I learned this: God is a gentleman and he is so patient. He waited for me to call on him and when I did, he was right there waiting for me to open my heart for him.

I called on Him, and a week later my friend, Ms. Jan Jacobs, gave me a beautiful bible Do you know that the acronym for the word BIBLE is *"Basic Instructions Before Leaving Earth."*

Somehow, I had to hit rock bottom emotionally and physically to ask for him to help. My journey to knowing Him began and my eyes were opened. I know that when I started to read the Bible, I realized he put me through this journey because of my sinful nature. This was the only way to prepare me for greater things in life. I am like a piece of clay that met the potter. He molded me and put me through the fire to bend and shape me into who I am today. Like this verse says:

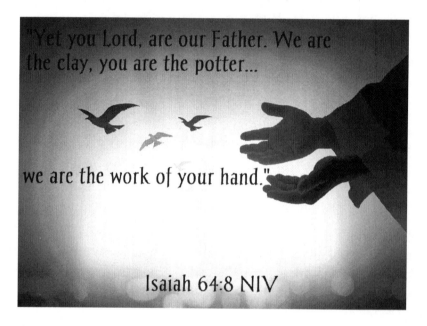

"Yet you Lord, are our Father. We are the clay, you are the potter...

we are the work of your hand."

Isaiah 64:8 NIV

First and foremost, always lean on God's word. Read His words and apply them to your life. Don't let our greed set in, stand strong on the good side and remember nothing good comes easy. Good things are worth fighting for. Work to build a strong work ethic by working in any job to build the skills and habits that lead you to build strong character. Hard work builds character, and when all is said and done, you too can say, "I've been there, and I know how you feel." When you give a lot, you gain a lot.

Hard work is the structure of life. Without it, we all will easily fall. My Father, Lord and Savior Jesus Christ is the architect of life, and when we let him, he builds us into a beautiful one-of-kind piece of art. The scriptures say that when you are obedient to the goodness of God, he will bless you.

"I sent you to reap what you have not worked for. Others have done the hard work, and you have reaped the benefits of their labor."   *John 4:38 NIV*

-4-

Gratitude

In life, gratitude is everything. It is like gasoline for your car, without it, we won't get very far. When we see someone, who is grateful for whatever they have, we will also see that they have a peaceful, joy-filled persona or demeanor about them. It's what most of us desire to have. Some of us don't know how to get it. Gratefulness gives us a better attitude towards life.

While my journey has not been fun, colorful, or beautiful, it is the journey I know best. As I've traveled on my life's journey, I've learned to focus on having the right attitude, and I am learning to let myself enjoy the journey. I will admit that sometimes my attitude needs some fixing before I can move forward, but that is ok, that is simply how life is. It is the journey I am meant to be on and one that will move me to keep striving to reach my goals.

During the most difficult times of my life, I know for certain that it was the attitude of gratitude that kept me alive. I had to learn to overcome the negative voices in my head as well as the negativity of what I was surrounded with. While it has taken diligence to not let those voices overtake me and make me succumb to bitterness, I have always known I would find a way.

During my life in the killing fields of Cambodia, everywhere I looked, people were starving to death. During the years that my little brother and I were alone and only had each other, we ate crickets, ant eggs, and whatever plants, fruits, and creatures we could scrounge up. We ate everything that was edible, except dead people.

Life was miserable.

As the days passed by, I became skin and bones covered with measles. It was not uncommon for my legs to swell with cuts and bruises and infected wounds. Often leeches would attach to my legs and suck on my wounds. And yet, as painful as it was, and despite being scared to death, I would venture into the pond to get water to drink for myself and my little brother.

I often wonder how a child at age seven or eight knew to boil the water before drinking it. I believe it was my nature to observe everything going on around me. I was very focused. Before our parents had been separated from us, I had watched them boil water in a tea kettle.

Later, by paying attention to everything around me, I learned to make a fire by rubbing rocks together. Then I used three bigger rocks to hold the pot, so I could cook the food we found, and boil our water. It is amazing how the will to live, to survive, comes from deep within. Those God-given skills are what He built inside of us and are what came to life and activated my senses in a time of need.

The Khmer Rouge took my parents away and they were gone for a very long time. I didn't know where they went. God must have had a bigger plan for my family because I have no other way to explain how we survived. As I interviewed my parents for this book, my mom shared that during the killing fields, the Khmer Rouge took her for questioning because she had a lighter complexion and looked Vietnamese. They questioned her about her ancestry, demanding the names of her family. She gave them the names and shared that she had some Chinese descent, along with a long bloodline of Cambodian ancestry, with most being farmers. She showed them the clothing she made, and they put her to work sewing straw hats.

Meanwhile, they assigned my father as the chief cook for the community. Suddenly, they sent him away, isolating him, interrogating him and making him work long hours in the fields. Even though his answers to their questions were the same as my mom's, they kept them separated. My father fell very ill and frail, and each day he fought to stay alive. He had no idea what happened to his family back in the village.

One occasion stands clearly in my memory. My brother was only about five years old. Because we had no clothes to wear, I had a torn-up rag of a sarong that I used to cover my female parts, but he had nothing. I could see his belly had grown huge on his skeleton of a body and his testicle was glowing like a lightbulb. I do not know how he lived.

We both had to grow up fast. Somehow, we were equipped with survival skills. I know kids these days would never have been able to survive.

Why do I bring gratefulness and attitude to this situation?

Well, I remember that my brother and I liked to climb trees after working in the rice fields. We played hide and seek, and I know that game saved my life! One day a big black buffalo came charging at me. My brother yelled out to me, screaming for me to climb up the very tree that we had been playing on. His horns missed me by a second. I remember laughing and crying at the same time.

I believe my fierce childhood saved me. I had to focus on one day at a time during that time. I just didn't have any other choice, but to find the best in the misery and hell that we were in. Laughing and playing never stopped. At that time laughing was all we had.

When we first came to America, my heaven, they put us in a two-bedroom, one-bathroom home that was very nice and clean. The home was right next to the railroad tracks that would wake us up every day at 5 AM in the morning. Our clothing was given to us by the church. Though everything was used, it was the best we had in many years.

The two bedrooms were too big for us, so we only used one room with our entire family sleeping on the floor surrounded by each other. A few months after we arrived, mattresses were sold to my parents by someone they called a friend. They were covered with nasty stains, and I believe he got them in the junkyard!

This man proved to be the devil in our lives. I believe that God shows us who they really are to help us learn who we should not be. While we are not to judge others, we can observe what others do, how they treat others, and how they live their lives. As I got older, I learned that while I do not have to like the person, nor be like that person, but that I should still show the love of God, even to our enemies. Unsavory people come into our lives as lessons that help us gain strength, grow, and not become complacent.

My parents are the kindest people on earth. I remember that once, on our way out of the killing fields as we were running toward Thailand, we had a little cart with wooden wheels that carried everything we owned, which was nothing more than a pot and a tea kettle. Yet, they would constantly stop and help others along the way who were in need.

When the twins were born in 1979, under the mango tree, my mom had nothing to wrap the babies in, so my dad took off his shirt and cut it in half to wrap each of them. We stayed under the mango tree for over three months. My dad had left us there in search of food. The three months he was gone seemed like three years. That mango tree covered us when it rained and from the sun. It gave us shelter when we needed it the most.

Each day that he was gone, I went looking for food. I went begging and even dug up the shallow graveyards to look for gold and jewelry. I somehow found a 2-3 carat ruby that was shining at me while I was searching. I traded that in for enough rice get us by for a while. Since we lived under the mango tree, we sure ate a lot of mangos!

Staying under the mango tree taught me valuable life lessons. The biggest lesson was about people. I realized that while some people are good and kind, not all are. Some who have more than others are often greedy and will not share.

I am so grateful to my dad. As I mentioned earlier, he was born into a poor, under-privileged family, whose mom gave birth to him and died seven days later. He was passed on to strangers to be cared for and became their property and lived as a servant. His education never went past seventh grade. Yet, in the way he lived his life, he taught by example and I was able to understand and recognize the good in life. My dad is the kindest, most joyful and happy man alive. He is not rich in money, but he is the richest man of all when it comes to what matters. He always has enough. While he had every right to complain about life, he found a way to be grateful and joyful every single day.

Not long after we moved to the U.S., my parents bought us a black and white TV from the flea market. I loved to watch "Tom and Jerry" cartoons in the morning before school. To stop the buzzing sounds on our TV and get a clear signal, we used foil to hold the antenna together. I liked that cartoon because I did not speak English, and Tom and Jerry didn't speak any words, there was a lot of silly action with them chasing each other. We were grateful for that little black and white TV set!

In a country of unfamiliarity, we needed each other and our freedom. My family was given an amazing opportunity to live in America. We are so grateful and appreciate the people that helped us on the way.

Life has a way of showing you who others are. I witnessed so many people that took advantage of others, and yet they did not get far in life. Why? Because if a person lives a life taking advantage of others, not only is it not a peaceful way to live, but everything one does will come back tenfold, either good or bad.

The best example of this is written about in the Bible. In Genesis Chapter 27, you can read the story of Jacob and Esau. In my understanding after reading that chapter, Jacob stole his brother Esau's identity and the blessing that belonged to him. Jacob paid the price for his sin, by running away, fearful that his brother would kill him. Then Jacob met Rachel, and fell in love with her, but couldn't marry her, even after working hard for seven years. He was hoping to marry Rachel, but he got tricked by her dad and ended up marrying Leah, the oldest sister, whom he had no interest in. When Jacob asked again, to take Rachel's hand in marriage, he had to work for seven more years to marry her.

That created so much chaos in that family. Sin doesn't let us get away without reaping the consequences. We must always listen to God's command. I know that not one of us on this planet is perfect and sinless, we all sin. The good part of our God is that when we repent of our sins and ask God for forgiveness, He blesses us with a new heart. Most people go through life without realizing anything is wrong and continue to sin. Our world has so many problems, due to the blame game going on, and no one takes responsibility for anything. Most people will only see what they want to see and most of the time they only see other people's problems rather than their own.

"Why do you look at the speck of sawdust in your brother's eye and pay no attention to the plank in your own eye? How can you say to your brother, 'Let me take the speck out of your eye,' when all the time there is a plank in your own eye? You hypocrite, first take the plank out of your own eye, and then you will see clearly to remove the speck from your brother's eye." Matthew 7:3-5 NIV

Having gratitude for our life and the experiences we endure puts us on a different path than other people. It allows us to see that no matter what we have, or don't have, we are blessed, thankful, and content for everything in life. We don't look at others and feel envy or jealousy. Gratitude helps us see the good in ourselves and others. In our nature, we tend to look at others and want what we don't have. We don't see the gift that God blessed us with.

We become unhappy and desire to have what other people have. We think that grass is greener on the other side. We forget to nurture our own gift. When we keep looking at others with envy and jealousy, we lose our happiness and joy from the inside--out.

The hardest part is staying in gratitude when we are hurting. I believe that when we are hurting, that is the time to plant our feet and simply be thankful for the situation you are in. From my own experiences, I have become a better person. The wisdom it has given me has enabled me to help my children and others around me.

Problems in life are just another way of testing us, helping us to become stronger and more resilient when handling the situations in our lives. Problems help build strength and make us stronger as humans.

We are like diamonds, that come in many colors and sizes. A Diamond comes from coal and the longer the coal has been subjected to extreme pressure and heat the better it crystallizes. It becomes a unique, colorless diamond, and it is priceless. When we go through life with extreme hardships and refuse to give up, we become a better person, just like those valuable diamonds. It is hard to find good diamonds that shine. If we choose not to grow through the tough times, we get stuck like coal before it became a diamond.

That is why I am grateful, and I don't like to complain about anything in my life. As you know misery loves company, and I don't want that type of company. I appreciate my journey and everything around me and know that my trials have made me a better human being.

People always say, "Sophal, you make everything look so easy. You are always so joyful and seem like you have no problems in your life." I believe that it is all about perspective. Yes, even after moving to America, I have had problems. But compared to the Killing Fields of Cambodia, I really don't have any problems. I left my problems behind. I would ask them, "What kind of problems do you have when you live in America?"

America is my heaven on earth. I have God, my family, and wonderful people around me. I have my soul and my freedom to do and believe in anything I want to believe and do whatever I want to do. I am free to be and act. I work hard, I make money and I can spend it anywhere, on anything I like to do. I don't have to worry about anyone taking my food, my home, and everything away from me. I have clean water to drink that I don't have to walk for miles to get it. I have plenty of good food to eat and clean clothes to wear. I have a clean bed to sleep in. As a matter of fact, it is so clean that I make sure my sheets and covers are super white. I have the ability to go to school and learn. I have the same freedom that often people in America are taking for granted.

"Anyone who listens to my teaching and follows it is wise, like a person who builds a house on solid rock. Though the rain comes in torrents and the floodwaters rise and the winds beat against that house, it won't collapse because it is built on bedrock. But anyone who hears my teaching and doesn't obey it is foolish, like a person who builds a house on sand. When the rains and floods come and the winds beat against that house, it will collapse with a mighty crash." When Jesus had finished saying these things, the crowds were amazed at his teaching, for he taught with real authority—quite unlike their teachers of religious law."   *Matthew 7: 24-29 NLT*

Now that I have a blessed life, it is hard for me to want to remember all the things that happened during my childhood. It is so emotional, and it is hard to have gratitude for this part of my life's story, but I know that without it I would not be where I am at today. I pray every second that I can keep moving forward and ask God to help me do so. Asking him to give me the wisdom that will help my readers to be touched, moved and inspired.

I thank God for all of it. The good, the bad, the ugly and everything in between. It is not fun, but through it all, I've learned so much, and no one can take it away from me. My prayer is to finish this book and impact others through my story, in the hopes that they too see God through my journey. He is there with me, and with them from the beginning to the end.

"When you have eaten and are satisfied, praise the Lord your God for the land he has given you."

DUETERONOMY 8:10 NIV

--5--

Love the Unlovable

Life can be tough, but when you add people that are not from the same culture or race, it can spell disaster. We eat differently, act differently, and come from different worlds. Each of us operates in our own individual world even though we live in the same place and location.

Most often, people stick to what they know. Of all the commandments in the Bible, the greatest command is Love. But, how do I love people who are from a different world than me? How do I apply love into my life? How do I love bad, mean, and cruel people? How do I learn to love myself?

When my journey of walking with God began in July of 2007, I found I had much to learn. I accepted that I was a dysfunctional sinful human, in need of a savior to help me escape the dark path that I was on. I learned that I was made in God's image and I needed to learn to love and understand myself, loving myself just as He loves me. That takes patience. I was never taught how to love, as all I knew was pain and suffering.

Upon reading the book of Galatians, I learned that I needed the fruit of the spirit to help me change me from the person that I was being. Coming to know God slowly began to give me the wisdom to know myself. That walk was not always easy, but I know that it is the only way to peace and the wisdom to discern what is going on in my life. God sent the people to show up in my life. That was the beginning of my journey. I'm still a work in progress.

Since sin entered humanity, we tend to be selfish and do things that are not pleasing to God. However, with the foundation of God's wisdom, we begin to operate within the mindset of love.

That foundation is God's wisdom and as I learned about His wisdom, I became better equipped to handle life's problems. We've all made many mistakes in life, and each of us is far from perfect. Probably the greatest sin is letting those mistakes tell us that we are unworthy of God's love. Yet, when I finally accepted the Lord Jesus Christ as my Savior, I noticed that every step I took led me to know Him and opened me to accepting wonderful new experiences. I met amazing Christian women to associate with, and as I grew in understanding and love I discovered "Bible Study International" where I was able to grow dramatically in a short few years. God continues to put knowledgeable skillful people in my life so that I can learn from them.

"And we know that God causes everything to work together for the good of those who love God and are called according to his purpose for them." Romans 8:28 NLT

When I decided to go back to school, I was accepted to Grand Canyon University (GCU), a Christian College. When I couldn't get my head wrapped around all the things that had happened in my life, God put me on another path, where I could more deeply understand all that has happened in my life.

Transformative learning came to me through Landmark

Education. It taught me that you can't access knowing from not knowing. I realized there is so many things that I do not know and that I have a huge blind spot.

"Be thankful in all circumstances, for this is God's will for you who belong to Christ Jesus."   1 Thessalonians 5:18

Through the ups and downs of my life I know I am saved by God's Amazing Grace. Learning to love who I am and that I am worthy of being loved by the God who created the universe. He made everything perfect. Wisdom is a blessing from God. Without wisdom, we have no direction and no peace.

God loves everyone on this earth so much that he sent his only son to die for us. All we must do is accept him into our heart. He loves us too much to leave us the way we were. We have a choice to either do God's way or choose to suffer our own way. God wants us to re-unite with him again like in the beginning. My morning prayer is for God to clean my heart, lead me to His way, and His will, and give me the wisdom to hear his voice and follow.

"Let the message about Christ, in all its richness, fill your lives. Teach and counsel each other with all the wisdom he gives. Sing psalms and hymns and spiritual songs to God with thankful hearts."
                                    Colossians 3:16 NLT

"But the fruit of the Spirit is love, joy, peace, forbearance, kindness, goodness, faithfulness, gentleness, and self-control. Against such things, there is no law."   Galatians 5:22-23 NIV

When it comes to marriage this scripture in Galatians is so important to remember. Marriage can be difficult and if you have two selfish people united in marriage, it can be the perfect recipe for disaster. It takes two people who really want to make it work. It is a commitment that requires both sides to give 100%. It is never 50/50. It will never work that way. If it is not 100% commitment you should never enter a relationship.

My husband and I both came from broken places, and we carried so many bags...way more than a Boeing 747 could carry! How do two imperfect people stay in love, long after lust and the initial glow of love has disappeared?

God led us to "Family Life Ministry" to get us to know him and learn from the examples of Godly people. Neither of us grew up with great role models on marriages. Although both our parents stuck together through good and tough times, I didn't see them express affection for each other. They are very old fashioned. Charles and I didn't truly have a peaceful marriage until we came to know God. Prior to my marriage to Charles, I had been married to a man that was all wrong for me. I had so much fear of loving or being loved by any man. Once we put God into the center of our marriage, we learned how to put each other's needs first. I feel so blessed that every step of the way, God led me to the place where I needed to learn and grow.

Now, I am delighted to say that the love we have for each other is stronger in all aspects than ever before. We are connected physically, emotionally, and spiritually. We pray that God continues to lead our lives and uses us to help others because we know the broken roads we once traveled. I love these verses from the Bible:

"Understand this, my dear brothers and sisters: You must all be quick to listen, slow to speak, and slow to get angry. Human anger does not produce the righteousness God desires. So, get rid of all the filth and evil in your lives, and humbly accept the word God has planted in your hearts, for it has the power to save your souls. But don't just listen to God's word. You must do what it says. Otherwise, you are only fooling yourselves. For if you listen to the word and don't obey, it is like glancing at your face in a mirror. You see yourself, walk away, and forget what you look like. But if you look carefully into the perfect law that sets you free, and if you do what it says and don't forget what you heard, then God will bless you for doing it."

James 1:19-25 NLT

Coming to understand God's word helps you to know your own self-worth and enables you to choose the right type of people to be around. For so many years I struggled with my own understanding of people. When it comes to loving someone, make sure to act and confront the problems that arise and not shut down. Love is not always sweet and cozy, it means that when life is difficult, take a stand for the person you love. Always communicate with love and affection.

Once you have experienced emotional and physical abuse and have taken action to leave a bad situation it is difficult to be open to and trust true love when it comes your way. Especially if you have had no role models. Remember that you must come to love yourself, just as God loves you, to be able to have a strong and wonderful relationship with a mate that is right and good for you.

In my Asian culture, love is not expressed in language. It shows through action. For example, cooking food and sharing fellowship with others is their love language. They don't say, "I love you", it is not normal for them to say I love you to their mates, let alone to their children. I never heard my mom and dad tell me they love me. I heard a lot of yelling and screaming, maybe because they had to work so hard to put a roof over our head and food on the table and they were exhausted and stressed. They were not educated to get good jobs here in the USA. The only jobs they could find were hard labor, at minimum wage. To make a living, they both had to work two jobs. Adding the language barriers, the only jobs they could find were blue-collar jobs.

I do understand their struggles more now, as an adult and as a parent. I feel true compassion and so much love for them. I could never thank them enough for being my parents. I think they did a great job with us five kids. The way we communicate together is not perfect but very authentic and full of love. My parents suffer from their own blind spots and it is my opinion they don't have the capability to grow out of their own world because they limited their life with the choices that they made.

With my parents, you'll never second guess what they are thinking. Their form of communication is yelling. You can literally hear them from ten blocks away. I grew up with that environment, but I do understand their love for us is more than any words could express. Their expression of love is that they like to cook special food for us. Their way of showing love is through what they do for us. As much as I love to eat, I am surprised that I am not 300 lbs.! I should be! Our communication with each other is a form of expressing unspoken love, sharing ideas, and being present in each other's world.

For anyone to see their blind spots, they must be in communication with other people. This helps us to expand our knowledge and understanding. We cannot isolate ourselves and expect to learn anything about others. We must be willing to be outside of our own world.

Being isolated, alone and mixing only with your own group, race, and community will not broaden your horizons and help you grow. That is why upon coming to America, my parents chose to live in Hummelstown, Pennsylvania. They wanted us to assimilate with other nationalities. We could have lived in Long Beach, CA where most of the Cambodian refugees resided, but that would not have served us well because we would have stayed in conditions that were largely familiar, surrounded by others who had also experienced harrowing loss, difficult times and grief.

Thank God for the wisdom and love of my parents. All five of us kids grew up to be decent, hardworking human beings. None of us got mixed with drugs or other damaging activities. Sometimes they seemed tough on us, but they taught us well. Despite their rough journey, they made sure they taught us many valuable life skills which have been a true blessing to each of us.

"Live in harmony with each other. Don't be too proud to enjoy the company of ordinary people. And don't think you know it all!" .... *Romans 12:16 NLT*

Growing up, as I dealt with my own emotions, recovering from the trauma of dark and difficult times in Cambodia, I often felt very alone even when I was surrounded by other people.

Often, I was unable to express myself freely or even fluently. When faced with difficult situations and unsure, I had to remove myself from the situation and learn to identify why I was feeling the way I was feeling. Whether I was angry, sad, scared or lonely, I had to learn how to process my feelings, let go and allow myself to heal. As I learned this, my life became much better because I learned how to be not only a better person but a better wife, friend, daughter, and mother.

We are called to love God and to love others, but how do we come to understand what love truly is? What does it mean to love yourself? What does loving someone really mean?

"But God demonstrates his own love to us in this: While we were still sinners, Christ died for us. Romans 5:8 NIV

"Dear friends, let us love one another, for love comes from God. Everyone who loves has been born of God and knows God. 1 John 4:7 NIV

There are many Bible verses that explain what love is. Following are just a few:

AHAB is a Hebrew word for love that describes a variety of intensely close emotional bonds. For example, Abraham loved his son Isaac (Gen. 22:2), Isaac loved his son Esau (Gen. 25:28), and "Israel loved Joseph more than all his children" (Gen. 37:3).

In a more romantic manner, Isaac loved his wife Rebekah (Gen. 24:67), Jacob loved Rachel (Gen. 29:18), and Delilah manipulated Samson by challenging his love for her. (Judg. 14:16)

We are all called to love the Lord, by expressing obedience to his commandments. (Duet. 6:5), and to "love thy neighbor as thyself" (Lev.19:18). Moreover, "He that getteth wisdom loveth his own soul." (Prov.19:8)

God's love is described well by the Greek word *AGAPAO*, which means unconditional love, preferential love that is chosen and acted out by the will. It is not love based on the goodness of the beloved, or upon natural affinity or emotion, rather it is benevolent love that always seeks the good of the beloved.

This type of love is exclusive to the Christian community because it flows directly from God's love:

"Beloved, let us love one another: for love is of God, and everyone that loveth is born of God and knoweth God. He that loveth not knoweth God, for God is love. 1 John 4:7,8

AGAPE love is a word that was common in both the Septuagint and the New Testament, however, the word rarely occurs in existing secular Greek manuscripts of the period. Like its synonym Philia, it designates love between persons (John 13:35), or people for God (1 John 2:15), of God for humanity (Rom. 5:8), and of God for Christ (John 17:26).

Whereas PHILIA emphasizes the idea of love arising from personal relationships, AGAPE is founded upon deep appreciation and high regard. It is perhaps for this reason that AGAPE is the love which God commands."

PHILEO is one of four Greek words for love, this one signifies friendship, fondness, affection, delight, and personal attachment.

This word is one of feeling – a heart of love – whereas AGAPE is a matter of benevolence, duty, and commitment. We are commanded to have AGAPE love (Matt. 5:44) but not PHILEO love because feelings cannot be commanded. PHILEO is also the word for "kiss." Jesus asked Peter if he had unconditional, sacrificial agape love, but Peter responded that he had Phileo or brotherly love. Peter's love deepened, and he wrote of agape love in his later books."

As for the love I have for my husband, can only be described by all three words that in Hebrew AHAB, AGAPAO, and PHILEO. When we disagree about something, I must remove myself out of the equation to put my thoughts in the right frame of mind. I must set everything else aside and pray for God's guidance. Putting everything else aside when we have a disagreement and pray that God works on me. If we don't learn to love in the way God loves us, we cannot love our mate.

When we love, it means taking the good, the bad, the ugly and everything in between. For example, my daughter Elisabeth has a mental disability and has special needs. Life with her is very hard and I will not lie, the struggle is real with her. Those who have a special needs child will relate to me. I never go anywhere without worrying that she is ok. She doesn't know how to take care of herself. When it comes to her care, I worry constantly whether the people taking care of her are good to her or not. Having a child with disabilities has affected the way I think, feel, and act. When we have social functions, I must decide if I should take her with me or not, and if I choose to take her with me, will she make people feel uncomfortable. Many times, she has accidents when she must go to the bathroom. It is very normal for people like her to have this issue, but I'm uncomfortable putting people who don't understand in an awkward position.

I'm not bringing this subject to this conversation with a victim mentality. I simply want people to be aware that there are people like myself who are caretakers for special needs loved ones and we care about what is going on in their world. I want people to discover that having a special needs child is a very special gift. I love my daughter so much and so many times I wish and pray for her to experience the normal life of a 24-year-old, but that is just a wish. She always shows me such unconditional love and there is never a day that Elisabeth comes home from her day program without greeting us with love.

As a young mother, I had to work so many jobs and had to depend on others to care for her. Often, I would feel so frustrated because I so hoped she would improve as she got older. I would be exhausted after working all day, then come home to cook, clean, do the laundry and worry about if my daughter is getting better. I honestly did not know how to love her until I learned about how God loves me. Now I know that God gave me Elisabeth to teach me love, patience, and understanding. To love someone that you don't get anything back in return is powerful. My Elisabeth is so loving and innocent. I know how blessed I am to have my daughter to help me to know how to love unconditionally.

As I reflect on my past, I often question why I married a guy like my ex-husband. Why I was not patient with my love life? Why didn't I wait? Why was I so stupid? I finally had to let it go. There are no good answers, it happened, and there is nothing I can do to change it.

I choose to love myself and my life's journey.

The greatest love God ever gave me is my children. I would have loved to be a stay at home mom and always be there for them. But that was not the way it was, yet I did the best that I could. Rather than beat myself up about my failures, I found that the better choice is to look at the failures in my life as valuable lessons to teach my children. Someone once told me, "failure is not a failure if you learn from it. Just don't make the same mistake twice!" God's love and wisdom have allowed me to help my children, to be their guard rail. I have enough experience to guide and help them make good decisions for their own lives. I realize that even with that they too will make their own mistakes, and I will love them through those times. It is life.

We all have genetic DNA to act on our own free will, they too must choose to listen, or not, and it is up to them.

As I was writing this chapter, my daughter Charlize is in her last year of high school. She told me she wanted to participate in this game that senior's in her High School call "senior assassin". I never heard of this kind of game and I have no idea how it works but, in my opinion, that's the most ridiculous game I had ever heard of.

I asked who came up with such an idea. I told her that I did not agree with it, and if she chooses to be involved in that activity, she would be involving herself with a selfish generation who only think about themselves. I encouraged her to stand on being different. I suggested that she do something different, like getting all the seniors together to do something great for the teachers, leaving a legacy for the next generation that comes after her. That ridiculous game will not help anyone.

What I was teaching her is that everything we do affects others and we need to think before we act. The name "senior assassin" alone does not sound right to me. I encouraged her to do the right thing rather than follow the crowd. I told her that as her mother I would support her for Godly actions, and it was time to make a positive imprint on her world. I told her that I believe in the possibility of her to accomplish great things.

"I give thanks to the Lord, for He is good! His faithful love endures Forever"

1 Chronicles 16: 34 NLT

I pray that each of my children come to know him as I do andthat they rely on him for everything in their lives. We must believe that all things will work out the way it should be as we put our best foot forward to do what we are supposed to do. In the midst of it all, trust in God for everything.

This is the time to love the unlovable. I stand for you!

"Trust in the Lord with all your heart; do not depend on your own understanding."   *Proverbs 3:5 NLT*

-6-

The Ability to Trust

When bad things happen, it is common to question how such a thing could happen, why it happened, and what was behind it all. Having seen and experienced so many bad things especially in my early years, I have done my fair share of questioning. The key for me has been how I have chosen to deal with not only the questions but the answers.

While my family was fleeing Cambodia, escaping to Thailand and the U.N. camps, we encountered minefields everywhere. We witnessed many people dying before our eyes, and their bodies were left where they fell.

It became "normal" because it happened so often. I could not feel anything any longer, I was numb to it because I had seen so much. It scared me that I felt that way.

When my father left to find food after my mom gave birth to my twin sisters under a mango tree, we had no food, water, clean clothing, or necessities that we simply take for granted today. We did have a few pots for cooking, but that was about it.

When my father did not return after a few days, we did not know where he was nor where to begin looking for him, even if we could have begun searching. We did not know if he was alive or had abandoned us.

Since I was the only one able to move around, I went in search of food so that my mother would have enough milk to feed the twins. I begged for food, to no avail. I searched for work in exchange for rice, but nothing was available. I then decided to dig the shallow graves to find jewelry worn by those who were killed by the Khmer Rouge.

Once, while doing this, I could no longer tolerate the smell of the dead bodies and was so frightened that I turned and was about to run when I discovered a 2-3 carat ruby. I traded it for ten cups of rice. That rice sustained us for a while.

My mom asked distant relatives if they would lend her some gold, which she would repay when my dad came back, but the answer was no. We scoured the jungle for edible fruits and vegetables scrounging for anything we could find.

Once, we encountered Vietnamese soldiers who were patrolling the Cambodian countryside and fortunately, mom knew how to speak their language. She explained our situation and they gave us food to eat.

After three very long months, my father returned. He had been collecting spring water and selling bottles of water to people traveling from Thailand to Cambodia. With that money, he was able to purchase sweet potato bread, cookies, and candies that did not get spoiled by the heat. With what little food he had, he shared it with the other refugees that likewise had nothing to eat.

Later, he explained why it had taken him so long to return to us. He had been to hell and back while he was away.

I admire my dad because nothing in life had ever been easy for him. As an orphan, he experienced many injustices as a youth. He always tells us even today that life is not about what happens to us, it is about what we do to overcome it. I have never seen my father dwell on the awful things that happened to him. He was and is always cheerful, hardworking, and very generous. He showed us that it is ok to trust others and let God decide who is good or who is bad. Some people would consider my father naïve, but his manner has always been to trust every person until they have proven him wrong.

When we came to America, we did not know English. I personally did not know how to describe my pain and what was going on in my mind, as I struggled to understand what had happened to my family and me. The more I tried to understand and figure out what had happened, the more it affected my mind and ability to act and even react.

As I grew up, I began to realize that sometimes ignorance is bliss. I felt that what I did not know, I simply did not know. I had no language to describe the pain I felt, so my survival mechanism was to replace pain with fun. I would joke and play around a lot so that I could deny pain. It took me away from my haunted memories.

Prior to 2007, when I learned about the Lord, Jesus Christ, I did not know how to trust and face life in the world I lived in.

- How do I make sense of my life?
- How do I trust a God that I had never seen?
- Why do bad things happen?

- Why do bad people exist?
- Deeper than that, why am I here on this earth?

I had so many questions, and up until that time, seemingly, no answers.

One day I began to read my Bible, and slowly I began to understand who God is. I believe that God purposely and intentionally picked me to go through the life journey that I have chosen to be on. The road I had chosen stems from what I know and feel.

I did not grow up with the word of God (the Bible). Nor did my family. Without the Bible, I was walking in darkness. When I began reading his word, it came alive within me. I prayed to him to help me open my heart and grant me the wisdom to know his voice and follow him.

God says in the Bible, *"My sheep listen to my voice; I know them, and they follow me."* John 10:27 NIV

"In the beginning was the Word, and the Word was with God, and the Word was God. He was with God in the beginning. Through him all things were made; without him, nothing was made that has been made. In him was life, and that life was the light of all mankind. The light shines in the darkness, and the darkness has not overcome it." John 1:1-5 NIV

How does trust play into this chapter of my life? I know now, that whatever happens from here on could never be worse than where I came from. I have learned to trust the wisdom God has instilled in me and know that He has my best interest in mind. I know that God's plan is always perfect, and He is good all the time.

Faith and Foundation

It is important to have a good foundation for life, such as God, family, and community. It has given me a sense of belonging and togetherness. My foundation had been shattered. I had quite a struggle to find who I am as a person. Growing up seeing torture and death as normal and the struggle of life is pretty much all I knew. Humans identify things in languages. I didn't even know how to identify anything in my life because I did not even know my own Khmer language properly, due to a lack of education. That solid foundation had been taken away from me at a very young age.

While children in America were starting school at the ages of four and five, I was struggling to survive. I did not begin to get an education of any kind until I came to America at fourteen years of age. I also did not have a manual, (the Bible) to guide me to living life in a way that pleases God, and therefore, I made my share of mistakes, especially in my early adulthood.

Since Studying my Bible, my life has not been the same.

God blessed me with good people so I can learn from them by their example of how to live a life of obedience. God also blessed me with bad people so I can learn not to be like them. I believe God instilled in all of us the sense of good and bad. The good is God. The bad is ourselves, which is our original sin. For us to overcome the bad, we have to work really hard. My original sin would be that I said, "I'm a sinner. God would never love a person like me. I am not good enough, and I can't do this, or that, or for that matter, write this book." I must overcome that voice. How did I do that? I took and continue to act on whatever I know that is good. I recently learned to identify the voice that keeps speaking negatively inside my head as my own machinery.

Keeping myself busy used to be the only way to keep my own machinery from taking me down. I no longer allow that to happen. That machinery is still there operating as usual in the background, but it has become powerless because I have learned to recognize it. Part of not understanding how to listen to my own inner voice could be that since I was a child of five, even till now, I have had no time to sit around and do nothing. Maybe that is why I did not hear the inner voice inside my head. Even today, I live a busy life, with work, school, raising a family, and life itself.

Now, as I expand my circle of people, I learn new things. One of the things I learned is about "Happy Hour." At the age of 25, one of my co-workers invited me to go to Happy Hour with her and I gladly accepted her invitation. What I learned is that if I did not like the environment I was in, I could change it. At the time, I was in a miserable marriage. The conversation that night made me realize that I was living in misery, and suddenly I was no longer afraid. If I had not gone to that Happy Hour, it may have taken me much longer to have the courage to leave the misery that I was in. Something in that conversation gave me the courage to become the person I wanted to be. I had to remove myself from the circle of my own people, my own community, and my own family to break free. I may have never learned about God and his plan if I had not been there that evening.

I took a leap of faith to overcome my own fear and scarcity mindset. To stretch beyond my comfort zone. If your own environment is toxic, know that it is like living in a community of crabs. If you take a bushel of crabs trying to escape a pot of hot water, none of them get out because each is pulling the other down. That is how it is with humans as well.

Since studying the Bible, I have come to understand that God wants the best for us. We as humans continue our own way and most of our ways are sinful. As humans, we have suffered from our own sins. Everything in life has consequences, either good or bad. Most of us only remember the goodness we do, but we don't want to remember the bad part of what we did. Everything we do affects people around us. If we can be mindful of our actions and take responsibility for our actions, maybe the world can be a peaceful place. As difficult life has been, I found it was also rewarding, as I learned and began to overcome my past.

I've learned to focus on the result and act on what I know is good. Good actions protect us from evil. During the time I was picking blueberries and living in the city of Philadelphia, I had to get up early every morning to catch the bus. I noticed that when people don't have anything to do, they tend to get themselves in trouble. They get hooked on drugs and alcohol, and many enter criminal activities.

The gift of work kept me out of trouble. Being busy working helped build great character and took my mind away from thinking or listening to the negative voices in my head. I put myself out there to do the work that I did not like to do, so I could gain the skills necessary to help me get to do what I like. Cleaning toilets, picking up trash, retail and professional jobs are all important because they represent the gifts that I was blessed with.

What I have learned is that when you build a strong work foundation, you know what it is like to work hard and build great character. Choosing to go through life sitting around and letting time pass you by, will not help you learn anything. You do not build your brain cells up to understand good solutions for living life.

From my observation, many of the younger generation are stuck in an entitlement mentality, expecting that the world should cater to their needs instead of putting themselves out there. Many have a foundation that is weak, and they are disconnected from the world they live in. They often complain, compare, compete with envy, and jealousy, leading them into a self-destructive spiral. Their minds become lazy and they begin gravitating towards things that are easy. I share this from my own experience. I have an adult son who refuses my advice. I have had to learn to allow him room to make his own way.

A broken foundation leads to so many problems and often passes from one generation to the next. At this point, I can only pray and ask God to lead him, and me to be obedient to his words.

I have to remind myself that God is in charge, that I have done all I can do, and all I can do is enough. Complaining about any situation in life is not going to change the situation. When people look at me, they think that I have no problems in life. That is simply not true. Believe me, there are many situations that come up in my life every single day just like everyone else. I just know not to complain about it. It's not going to do me any good. I also realized the more I do things without complaining, the more God will entrust me with new tasks to take on to get me closer to my goal in whatever I set for. Any task I was able to overcome, He will reward me with a new level.

"Whoever can be trusted with very little can also be trusted with much, and whoever is dishonest with very little will also be dishonest with much."   Luke 16:10 NIV

The older I am, the more I own my truth. This is the only way I can start to build a stronger foundation for myself and the next generation to come. I've learned to have faith in people and give people the benefit of the doubt until they prove me wrong. I know that no one on this planet is sinless.

Do you know anyone that is sinless? The only person that I know who is sinless is Jesus. He was born over two thousand years ago, and at the age of 33, he offered his life to save us. I encourage you to read the Bible it will give you the understanding of what I am talking about more clearly from your own heart. I want people to have a relationship with God like I have, and it starts with reading his word. Although the devil knows the Bible inside and out, he chose to follow his own heart.

The distinction between the devil and the true believer of Jesus Christ is that we are willing to change. We are willing to ask for forgiveness and repentance of our sins. That is when

God starts working on our hearts, and, at that moment, we will see the difference in our lives. For those who know the words and don't come to repentance and submit their hearts to God, they will not change.

Have you heard this before? *"The definition of insanity is doing the same thing over and over and expecting different results."* That is for those who know the words of God and don't change. In order to change, you must take action to change.

Think of the process of you deciding to do something good. There is always something that stops you from getting where you want to be, so you must be strong. Learn to identify your weaknesses. Your inner voice is not your friend most of the time. It's always talking you out of doing something good.

If I let my inner voice take over, I would not be able to get up. My inner voice would be saying something like this... "you are sinner, you don't deserve God's forgiveness, why don't you just go bury yourself, or even worse, just jump off a bridge." It was several years into my coming to have faith in my Lord Jesus Christ when I cried out to him confessing my sin regarding thinking of taking such an action. I needed God to tell another human being to tell me that I was forgiven. The thoughts in my head keep saying, "Why do you think God would forgive you?"

One Sunday morning we went to the Frederick Christian Fellowship Church, in the town we lived in, Frederick Maryland. That morning, Pastor Randy said this before he started his sermon, "If someone feels that God has not forgiven you, I want you to know that He did." While he was saying that, he looked directly at me, as I was sitting in the front row.

From then on, I continue to cry out to God for all my problems. Yes, there are times that I forget to take my problems to him because of being busy, but I always come back to having my conversations with God. The more I stay in God's word I know I am ok. Living in a world surrounded by non-believers makes it easy to second guess yourself. I often do that. Every day, I start with my devotion to fill my day with Faith. God's words help me not to listen to my inner voice. The one that says I am not good enough.

The more I study His word the more I feel that I am standing on a solid foundation. It is like building a house of brick, not straw or sand. I want a rock-solid home that is not shaken by any storm. I believe God put me in the path where he will help me to strengthen my weaknesses so I can do the work that he set out for me.

When I have my morning with God, I feel better and I am more equipped to face my own fears. The more I consistently read God's Word, which has become my comfort food, the better my life is and the more I'm blessed with good people and situations who support my journey.

> *"Now faith is confidence in what we hope for and assurance about what we do not see."*   *Hebrews 11:1 NIV*

I have faith in God, that He can change my heart. Definition of Faith is "In one sense, faith in Christianity is often discussed in terms of believing God's promises, trusting in his faithfulness, and relying on God's character and faithfulness to act."

If you say you have faith in God and you don't act on doing good, you are not living in faith. I heard someone mention this before to me *"faith without action is dead faith"*.

"For it is by grace you have been saved, through faith...and this is not from yourselves, it is a gift of God." Ephesians 2:8

After I acknowledged that God had forgiven me, I believe that He is the one who is giving me the wisdom each day to know how to discern what is coming at me, and the ability to follow him. My prayer every morning is that he gives me a fresh start for my day, the wisdom to be conscious and the obedience to listen to his directions.

As a Christian, God commands us to love one another. He commands us to love our enemy. He doesn't say you have to be co-mingled with them and be like them. I also know God forgave me of my sins, and as I am also a sinner and guilty like everyone else, I need to forgive them for hurting me. My life's purpose is to live a full life of love for others. If I am not loving, then I can't stand up for the goodness of God. I would be a hypocrite.

Because I call myself a Christian, I must love all people, even my enemy. I don't have to like what they do, nor do I have to associate with them, I simply need to stand with the truth and be the light for them to see their way home. I know God's truth will set us free. God's truth opens the door to show them love and I can be the light for them to find their way out of the darkness. As we all know we all will die one day, we just don't know when. How do we want to live our lives? I want to make a difference in people's lives.

"For the wages of sin is death, but the gift of God is... Eternal Life in Christ Jesus our Lord."

Romans 6:23 NIV

I look back at my life growing up without God. I was judgmental and was not at peace with myself. That's because of the shattered broken foundation. I continue to witness so much pain and suffering going on in the world and I realize that so many people on this planet are broken too. I want to share with others about my own broken foundation so that they can learn to repair their own foundation and start with a new and fresh foundation for themselves. I am now more mindful and present to living my life.

When I observe everyone on this planet as an individual, or a group, a race, an ethnicity, I ask: "Who are we to say who is better than who?" We are not God. The world we live in is so quick to judge others. That is why we have so many problems around the world. Knowing that we are all broken, gives us a reason to accept a God who can help repair us and put us back into the perfect place where we should be.

-8-

His Grace is Sufficient

You ask, "why me?" I say, "Why not me?" I was born in a place called "Cambodia" in the midst of fighting and chaos, growing up in that country that became known to the world as "The Killing Fields." I barely survived all of that! But I did, by the grace of God.

While thinking about the ending of this book I was lying next to my husband. The tears ran down my face into my ears because I reflected on the past and I was so overwhelmed with joy. I realized how blessed and loved I am by an amazing God. I live in Scottsdale AZ. I'm learning God's words, hearing and understanding Him. The book of Romans revives me by grace through faith. Each day God has shaped and sculpted me to be more like Him. Through the midst of the storm I'm not shaken, I'm at peace because I know who my father is. He is my Lord Jesus Christ.

As I look back on it all I now understand and believe it all in God's perfect plan for me. I understand that there is grace for me from God. He has forgiven me for my sins although I don't deserve it. Who am I to judge, hold a grudge and not be forgiving? I realized that everyone is perfect just the way they are.

I suffered at the hands of broken people who did not know the love of God and suffered from a scarcity mindset. I forgive them as I have been forgiven. For it is not my place to judge nor persecute them for I am not God.

His grace is enough, and it has left me feeling peace, joy, and happiness. You might describe these things of beatitude which refer to a state of great joy.

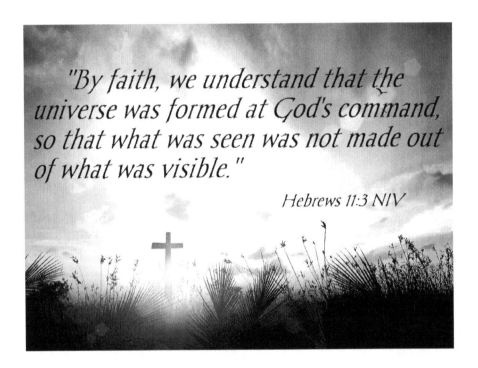

"By faith, we understand that the universe was formed at God's command, so that what was seen was not made out of what was visible."

Hebrews 11:3 NIV

Interviews

I interviewed some of my family members who had completely different experiences in life since they were born after the invasion. They did not go through the war but have stood by and loved the ones who did.

This is from my baby sister, Daisy Nop.

What has it been like to be in a family who went through such trauma?

To be honest, it's been a blessing in disguise for me. I know it sounds awkward or insensitive to say, but I can explain. As for me I am the youngest of the five siblings, so I knew nothing about the war, nor did I go through the hardships that my parents and my entire family had to endure through the trauma of the Khmer Genocide. Until I was older like around 6 or 7 years old that's when I had an idea of what my family went through then I realized how BLESSED I was to be a part of this family who survived this horrendous genocide.

I look back and wonder, how in the world did my parents, oldest sister, and brother survive this war because many families were split up or executed right on the spot! Only one answer comes to my mind and it is our Heavenly Father who pulled us all through this war. So many people have died, family members split up or unknown casualties...and somehow God has saved all 7 members of our immediate family!

How blessed are we to be able to survive and live this journey to America and start a new chapter with all surviving family members intact! I call that Blessed and saved by Grace and Mercy from the Almighty God! Often when life doesn't go as planned and we go through traumatic situations in life, we ask and wonder if God has abandoned us through these hard times, but we must trust that God's providence will work through it.

The Providence of God has set things up so that what he wants to happen will happen. The truth is, that he positioned us right where we are today. God truly has a purpose and a plan for our family even through the trauma that he used for the good! When we are obedient and trust in Him, we can be a blessing to others by inspiring through our stories!

My point in saying all this is that I believe that God set-up the timeline of events in my oldest sister's (Sophal) life to allow her to share her story so that it can bring hope, faith, trust and love to the world! I have nothing but gratitude for my family and every day I am grateful to be alive! When your family goes through this type of trauma you have nothing but gratitude in any type of situation!

How has it impacted your life?

As a result of the trauma, it has impacted my life growing up in America as a 2nd generation Khmer American. The impact was more positive than negative, but ultimately, we chose the path of our journey! For example, it has built a lot of character, courage, and strength in our immediate family. My oldest sister and brother paved a way for us learning life skills in an environment of hard work, grit, and patience.

It has given me a better perspective on why my parents do the things they do. Some examples are the way they've raised all of us, communicate to us, and how they show us love in a different way. Culturally, most older generations express love in more passive-aggressive ways, but we've learned to show love differently to our kids. We've learned to parent in a more straightforward, affectionate and authentic manner. It has impacted the way I decide to do things in life because I've gained a better knowledge of the roles I play in my daily life as a sister, daughter, wife, mother, and friend.

What my family experienced has had an impact on our relationships, but in the end, we've chosen the best roles in our lives! I have a second mother in my oldest sister which had a major impact on not only my life but that of my siblings. It was her responsibility to care for us while my parents worked to earn a living.

Sophal's influence and care made such a difference as to how I viewed life. She taught by example, that no matter how tough life can be, you never give up. She's been through so much, and yet, I never saw her give up on herself! When she's fallen, she has gotten right back up and moved forward in her journey! Babysitting her kids through my teen years had a positive impact on me as well, as it prepared me to be the mother I am today. I now have children and am grateful to have had those responsibilities growing up around my oldest sister!

Finances were tight growing up, which impacted our lives, but didn't impact our outcome! The hardships and experiences did start us out with humble beginnings but paved the way for a successful future. When we find our lives in the middle of messy situations, we have to remember that we live this life for a purpose and that is to impact others in a positive way!

True, our situation was difficult because our family had to start over in America with nothing, and not understanding the English language was a big barrier. Being the only Asian family, in the 1980s in small-town Hummelstown, PA with most of the population being Caucasian, made us a target for bullies and racism and had an impact on each of our lives. We certainly had to develop thick skins to endure the racial intolerance!

What have been your greatest challenges in supporting your loved one through painful memories and trauma?

My greatest challenge has been knowing that I can't take away the pain, memories, nor traumatic experiences that my family endured during the war. To see the resiliency of my oldest sister bouncing back to life and moving forward has been incredible to witness. Communication was a big challenge because without having experienced those things myself, it is difficult to fathom and understand, even when they shared their stories. For so long, I did not understand their pain because I did not understand the origins of the pain.

What would you say to others who likewise play a supportive role for trauma victims?

To be an encouragement for them mentally and spiritually and to provide a strong support system for them when they need you most. So, choose your circle wisely and intentionally! In this journey of life, we need each other. We were never meant to do life alone! I try my best to be there for my older sister when she needs me and to be a good listener, without judgment and with empathy.

What qualities did being in a supportive role develop for you?

Optimism, diligence, hopefulness, faithfulness, positivity, loyalty, and a strong bond with my oldest sister. Just witnessing the trauma that my loved ones had to go through made me more confident in the unconditional love that God has for all of us and helped make wiser choices in life and build meaningful relationships with loved ones that will last forever. There's an old Zambian proverb that says, *"When you run alone, you run fast. But when you run together, you run far."* Life is not a 50-yard dash; it's a marathon!

Daisy Nop

This next one is from my sister Sophia, (Pia)

What has it been like to be in a family who went through such trauma?

Being a part of a family that went through such trauma, makes it harder and more difficult to communicate your feelings. My parents weren't expressive, nor did they ever ask us to express ourselves freely. Instead, we held our feelings inside not knowing how to express ourselves effectively. Due to that, it was easy to become passive-aggressive, because even though you want to communicate your feelings and tell your family members how you really feel, you are afraid of how they would react, or do not know how they will react. You don't want to hurt their feelings considering all the traumas they've experienced in Cambodia.

This resulted in a lot of hurts, pains and trauma seeping up and causing huge fights or arguments over other things that happened in the family. My parents are resentful and bitter people through their words and actions, and when there are issues that need to be resolved, they will not address the specific issue but instead, avoid the actual conflict by bringing up past actions or wrongdoings against you. They have not buried the past, it always shows up when there are hurt feelings or conflicts in our family. Sometimes, these learned behaviors are transferred into my own interactions with my spouse and child and I've learned to step back and evaluate my behavior and own up to it.

How has it impacted your life?

I know the past and how you grew up does not define you and who you are now; but growing up in a family that had members who experienced such a traumatic event (i.e. Pol Pot camp), it has impacted my life in a significant way – both in the negative and positive aspects. Mainly, I see it in how we deal with conflict resolutions in our family but in other ways, it has impacted my life in a positive way as well.

On the positive side, because I wasn't entitled to things, spoiled by a privileged life or given things freely, I learned to work hard and respect the value of hard work. I gained a better work ethic. Also, I became a resilient, tough person, adjusting/transitioning well to the difficult situation that life has brought me. The negative impact on me growing up were things like looking at your peers at school with envy because their parents are "involved" in their academics and social lives, attending their sports game, school events, and that they had nice, big homes, new clothes, etc.

As a kid, I didn't understand why we didn't have the things that other American families had and was filled with envy and sadness. I understand now as an adult, all the sacrifices and hard work my parents and my older siblings, Sophal and Soup have made so that I could become the person I am now. As an adult, you learn from your past and you choose not to dwell on your past. But you can use your past experiences (both the negative and positive) as a learning tool to become a better human being who is filled with love, grace, and gratitude for your family.

What have been your greatest challenges in supporting your loved one through painful memories and trauma?

The greatest challenge has been in the area of communicating our feelings with one another. Although communication has gotten better amongst our siblings, it is still difficult communicating well with my parents. Mainly, we get lost in our translations and our perspectives are different. Being completely honest with one another is difficult during family conflicts. For example, being brutally honest with an over-bearing, stubborn mother has gotten me nowhere with her and the more I engage, the more frustrating it is. The last time I thought I was being honest with her, resulted in her screaming at me and accusing me of being disrespectful of her parental authority. The only way to deal with our mom is to retreat and throw up your white flag. She is set in her ways and she does not want to be told what to do or how to feel; let alone, "disrespect" her with our honesty.

When conflicts arise within our family, she is quick to call the faults, blame others and play the victim, rather than just telling them that you disagree with their choices, or feel frustrated, or privately tell each other that they have hurt the other. It has gotten a lot better through the years as we experience God's grace and have a deeper understanding of God's love. Before, it was hard to feel like your family loved you and supported you no matter what happened.

It has changed for the better now that we have gotten older and realize that we no longer have the luxury of time; it's precious and we don't want to waste time with our small, petty quarrels.

What would you say to others who likewise play a supportive role in trauma victims?

Continue to love them, practice empathy daily and support your family members no matter the circumstance. I feel like people want to know and have affirmation from their loved ones that they are doing OK and that they are loved and cared for.

What qualities did being in a supportive role develop for you?

Qualities that developed through the years in this supportive role have been learning how to adjust quickly to difficult situations, becoming more understanding with my family members by being a better listener and not quick to comment/react right away. Because I was never seen as an outspoken person, I have had people tell me that I'm a "passive" person. Being viewed as a passive person frustrated me and hurt my feelings. I've learned to speak up for what is right and to not become a "passive-aggressive" person. Growing up in a family like mine, you learn to become tough as nails. Finally, you never take anything or anyone for granted.

Final Thoughts

On June 26th, 2007, my transformation started by reading the BIBLE. It was the beginning of the healing process of my heart and forgiveness. Then, in the complete healing of my journey, another greater transformation came to me in January 2019. My husband enrolled me in "Landmark Forum", and I had faith enough to attend. That journey healed my head. I believe nothing in life happens by accident. This is by design from my Heavenly Father. God transformed my heart and he used the Landmark Methodology to help transform my head so that I have the skill to help others to not be stuck on the past, and let the past be just what it is...the past.

Landmark put me in the position of realizing that everyone has problems, big and small and those problems traumatize them on different levels and influence how each handles life's problems. It does not matter whether you live in America or in Asia, we all have problems. It is inherently a part of life from the time we are born. But until we begin following the manual, and are willing to be obedient to it, we will continue to sin and hurt others.

That is unnecessary. We can share with others how to live better and show them the way. Yes, it is easier said than done. I myself have no desire to carry the weight of the past because it does not serve me. There is a sermon I have heard many times that says, "when you hold a grudge against someone, and cannot forgive, it is like drinking the poison yourself and expecting them to die." I have learned not to carry my invisible baggage any longer.

What is Landmark? "The Landmark Forum is designed to

bring about positive, permanent shifts in the quality of your life—in just three days. These shifts are the direct cause of a new and unique kind of freedom and power—the freedom to be at ease and the power to be effective in the areas that matter most to you: the quality of your relationships, the confidence with which you live your life, your personal productivity, your experience of the difference you make, your enjoyment of life."

I would say this is much more effective than going to see the psychiatrist. This experience affects everyone differently. In my opinion, because I have gone through learning the Bible and took classes at GCU on the Christian Worldview, I have a better understanding of how God is using me in this journey. I am much more understanding of people and have a higher view of God. I know my purpose in life. As Mark Twain said: *"The two most important days in your life are the day you are born and the day you find out why."*

Everything in life matters to God. He uses all kinds of tools to help me to be the person he designed me to be, but it only helps if I choose to use them, and I am willing to work on my future. Because of my sinful nature, I need to work hard on myself so that I don't continue to sin. I also know that because I am not perfect, I will continue to make mistakes, and that is ok.

In all my actions in life, I took a leap of faith never to let the negative things put me on a path that is not good for me and the people around me. My Faith resides in the God that I have never seen, but who I believe in, and I know that everything will be ok.

Most people stop trying because they just don't believe in themselves enough. They too can change, and the biggest enemy is themselves.

About the Author

Sophal Pettit

Sophal was born in Takeo, Cambodia, a small town near the Vietnamese border on July 16th, 1970. At the tender age of five, the Khmer Rouge, a communist guerrilla group led by Pol Pot, took power in Phnom Penh, the capital of Cambodia forcing all city dwellers into the countryside and labor camps. During their rule, it is estimated that nearly 2 million Cambodians died by starvation, torture or execution. Having survived the horrible suffering and nightmares of the killing fields, at the very young age of fourteen, she and her family of seven arrived in the United States as refugees.

Beginning life anew in Hummelstown, PA was not without its

challenges. Having never had a formal education, she entered school for the first time at age fourteen, without knowing a word of English, an Asian child in a classroom of white children, who, having heard their parents talk of the Vietnam war, did not take kindly to someone so different from themselves.

Struggling to adjust in a new country and culture, life was full of hard work, and new, often difficult experiences. Married at a young age, Sophal's life took a new twist, as her abusive alcoholic husband wreaked havoc on the lives of her and her children. Finally, she and her children escaped the abusive marriage, and hard work, determination, and a will to survive spurred her forward.

In 1997, Sophal met and married her husband Charles, and together they began building both their lives and business together. In July of 2007, with changing economic times, business failure looming and her health failing, exhausted and disillusioned, Sophal found God. The transformation it brought to her life and the lives of her family is exceptional. In her journey of self-discovery, her faith, gratitude and trust in her wise and loving God has brought her a fulfilling and joy-filled life that she shares with all she meets.

Sophal's touching powerful personal story will touch and inspire you and demonstrates her unfailing mindset that her life is destined for success.